PEARL CLEAGE

Pearl Cleage (she/her/hers) is an Atlanta-based writer who is currently Distinguished Artist in Residence at the Alliance Theatre. She was appointed Atlanta's first Poet Laureate in 2020. Her plays include *Flyin' West*, *Blues for an Alabama Sky* and *Bourbon at the Border*, commissioned and directed by Kenny Leon at the Alliance Theatre. She is also the author of *A Song for Coretta*, written in 2007 during Cleage's time as Cosby Professor in Women's Studies at Spelman College. Her play *The Nacirema Society Requests the Honor of Your Presence at A Celebration of Their First One Hundred Years* was commissioned by the Alabama Shakespeare Festival and premiered in the fall of 2010, in a joint production by the ASF and Atlanta's Alliance Theatre, directed by Susan Booth. Her plays have also been performed at Arena Stage, Hartford Stage, the Oregon Shakespeare Festival, the Huntington Theatre, the Alabama Shakespeare Festival, the Long Wharf Theatre, Just Us Theatre, True Colors Theatre, Bushfire Theatre, the Intiman Theatre, St Louis Black Repertory Company and Seven Stages. She is also an accomplished performance artist, often working in collaboration with her husband, writer Zaron W. Burnett, Jr. They have performed at the National Black Arts Festival, the National Black Theatre Festival, and colleges and universities across the country. Cleage's most recent play, *Angry, Raucous and Shamelessly Gorgeous*, premiered at the Alliance in 2019, directed by Susan Booth, and recently completed a run at Hartford Stage. She has recently been commissioned by Fords Theatre as part of their Lincoln Legacy Project to create *Something Moving: A Meditation on Maynard*.

Cleage is also an accomplished novelist. Her novels include *What Looks Like Crazy On An Ordinary Day*, a *New York Times* bestseller and an Oprah Book Club selection, *I Wish I Had A Red Dress*, *Some Things I Never Thought I'd Do*, *Babylon Sisters*, *Baby Brother's Blues* and *Seen It All and Done the Rest*. She also has written *Till You Hear From Me* (Ballantine/One World) and is the author of *Mad at Miles: A Blackwoman's Guide to Truth*, a groundbreaking work of race and gender, along with *We Speak Your Names*, a praise poem commissioned by Oprah Winfrey for her 2005 celebration of legendary African American women and written in collaboration with Zaron Burnett. Cleage has also written for magazines, including *Essence*, *Vibe*, *Rap Pages* and *Ms*. In addition to her work as the founding editor of *Catalyst* magazine, a literary journal, she was a regular columnist for the *Atlanta Tribune* for ten years, winning many awards for her thought-provoking columns. She has also written for TheDefendersOnLine.com. Cleage has been awarded grants in support of her work from the National Endowment for the Arts, the Fulton County Arts Council, the Georgia Council on the Arts, the Atlanta Bureau of Cultural Affairs and the Coca-Cola Foundation. Her work has earned her many awards and honours, including an NAACP Image Award for fiction in 2008.

pearlcleage.net

Pearl Cleage

BLUES FOR AN ALABAMA SKY

NICK HERN BOOKS
London
www.nickhernbooks.co.uk

A Nick Hern Book

Blues for an Alabama Sky first published in Great Britain in 2022 as a paperback original by Nick Hern Books Limited, The Glasshouse, 49a Goldhawk Road, London W12 8QP, by special arrangement with Theatre Communications Group, Inc., New York

Cover photograph of Samira Wiley (in the 2022 National Theatre production) by Juco

Designed and typeset by Nick Hern Books, London
Printed in the UK by Mimeo Ltd, Huntingdon, Cambridgeshire PE29 6XX

A CIP catalogue record for this book is available from the British Library

ISBN 978 1 83904 099 3

Woodland
CARBON
www.woodlandcarbon.co.uk
NICK HERN BOOKS
Printed on Carbon Captured paper

Blues for an Alabama Sky was originally commissioned by the Alliance Theatre Company in Atlanta, Georgia (Kenny Leon, Artistic Director; Edith H. Love, Managing Director), where it premiered in July 1995. The production subsequently returned to Atlanta as part of the Culural Olympiad, in conjunction with the Olympic Games in the summer of 1996. The cast was as follows:

ANGEL ALLEN	Phylicia Rashad
GUY JACOBS	Mark C. Young
DELIA PATTERSON	Deidrie N. Henry
SAM THOMAS	Bill Nunn
LELAND CUNNINGHAM	Gary Yates

Director	Kenny Leon
Set Designer	Rochelle Barker
Lighting Designer	Judy Zanotti
Costumer Designer	Susan E. Mickey
Sound Designer	Brian Kettler
Musical Composition	Dwight Andrews

Blues for an Alabama Sky was revived in the Lyttelton auditorium of the National Theatre, London, on 27 September 2022 (previews from 20 September). The cast, in order of speaking, was as follows:

ANGEL ALLEN   Samira Wiley
GUY JACOBS   Giles Terera
LELAND CUNNINGHAM   Osy Ikhile
DELIA PATTERSON   Ronkę Adékoluęjo
SAM THOMAS   Sule Rimi
ENSEMBLE   Lincoln Conway
                             Eddie Elliott
                             Kimberley Okoye
                             Helena Pipe

Understudies
ANGEL ALLEN   Helena Pipe
GUY JACOBS   Eddie Elliott
LELAND CUNNINGHAM/
   SAM THOMAS   Lincoln Conway
DELIA PATTERSON   Kimberley Okoye

Director   Lynette Linton
Set and Costume Designer   Frankie Bradshaw
Lighting Designer   Oliver Fenwick
Composer   Benjamin Kwasi Burrell
Sound Designer   George Dennis
Movement Director   Kane Husbands
Wigs, Hair
   and Make-up Designer   Cynthia De La Rosa
Company Voice
   and Dialect Coach   Hazel Holder
Drama Therapist   Wabriya King
Staff Director   TD. Moyo

Producer   Fran Miller
Production Manager   Anna Fox
Casting   Alastair Coomer CDG
                             and Chloe Blake
Dramaturg   Nina Steiger
Stage Manager   Ian Farmery
Deputy Stage Manager   Anna Sheard
Assistant Stage Manager   Shaneice Brown

Characters

ANGEL ALLEN, *a thirty-four-year-old black woman who looks
    five years younger, former back-up singer at the Cotton Club*
GUY JACOBS, *a thirty-ish black man, costume designer at the
    Cotton Club*
DELIA PATTERSON, *a twenty-five-year-old black woman,
    social worker on staff at the Margaret Sanger family
    planning clinic*
SAM THOMAS, *a forty-year-old black doctor at Harlem
    Hospital*
LELAND CUNNINGHAM, *a twenty-eight-year-old black man
    from Alabama, a six-week resident of Harlem*

Time and Place

It is the summer of 1930 in Harlem, New York.

The creative euphoria of the Harlem Renaissance has given way
to the harsher realities of the Great Depression. Young
Reverend Adam Clayton Powell, Jr. is feeding the hungry and
preaching an activist gospel at Abyssinian Baptist Church.
Black Nationalist visionary Marcus Garvey has been discredited
and deported. Birth-control pioneer Margaret Sanger is opening
a new family planning clinic on 126th Street, and the doctors at
Harlem Hospital are scrambling to care for a population whose
most deadly disease is poverty. But, far from Harlem, African-
American expatriate extraordinaire, Josephine Baker sips
champagne in her dressing room at the Folies Bergère and
laughs like a free woman.

Setting

The setting is an apartment building in Harlem. Three of the characters occupy two apartments which are across the hall from each other. There is a lot of running between apartments and access to and fro should be so easy that at times it seems to be one large living space.

Guy's apartment is slightly larger than Delia's and should have a couch large enough for someone to lie down on. In one corner of the room is a sewing area. It has a sewing machine, a woman's dress form, a full-length mirror, pieces of fabric, sewing supplies and a crowded clothes rack. This corner is Guy's workspace and is off-limits to others. In contrast to the congenial clutter of the rest of the apartment, this space is efficiently organized. On the wall, there is a large photograph of Josephine Baker. She is smiling broadly. There is a door opening to the bedroom, which is unseen.

Delia's apartment is a small studio. There is a small table with two chairs and a tiny bookcase full to bursting with books and pamphlets. A door opens to a bedroom which is unseen.

Both apartments have small hot plates, but no kitchens.

There should also be a window facing the street from the larger apartment so that characters can talk out the window to people in the street area.

ACT ONE
Scene One: Sunday morning, 3 a.m.
Scene Two: Sunday, late afternoon
Scene Three: Wednesday, late afternoon
Scene Four: Sunday evening
Scene Five: Friday evening

ACT TWO
Scene One: two weeks later, Sunday afternoon
Scene Two: two weeks later
Scene Three: the next day
Scene Four: the next day
Scene Five: two weeks later

ACT ONE

Scene One

Sunday morning, 3 a.m. The street is quiet. Suddenly, there is the sound of two people half-dragging, half-carrying a third. GUY and LELAND enter on each side of a loudly drunken ANGEL.

ANGEL. I can't believe it. I just can't believe it. I... can... not... believe... it. Can you believe it?

GUY (*struggling to keep* ANGEL *on her feet*). I can't believe it.

ANGEL. Me either! I can't believe it!

She stumbles. LELAND *catches her.*

Damn!

GUY. Home at last! Thank God. And thank you, brother. I don't think we would have made it that last two blocks without you!

LELAND. Is she sick?

GUY (*surprised at the question*). She's drunk!

ANGEL (*indignant*). And so what? If you can't be drunk in Harlem, where the hell can you be drunk? Besides, we're celebrating, aren't we?

GUY. Of course we are, Angel. (*To* LELAND.) Thanks again, Ace. I think I can take it from here.

ANGEL. Tell him why we're celebrating. (*To* LELAND.) Did he tell you why we're celebrating?

LELAND. No, he...

ANGEL. And I didn't tell you, did I?

GUY. Don't answer. You'll just encourage her.

ANGEL. Did I?

LELAND. No, you...

ANGEL. So, tell him, Guy. He has a right to know. Don't you think you have the right to know?

LELAND. I don't want to...

ANGEL. Of course you do. Tell him.

GUY. And then will you come upstairs before you wake up the whole building?

ANGEL (*drunkenly indignant*). They need to wake up! Negroes sleeping their damn lives away. (*Screams.*) Wake up!

GUY. Hush, girl! You gonna get us all evicted.

ANGEL. Then tell him.

GUY. Her gangster just dumped her. So she's celebrating.

ANGEL. He's not a gangster. He's a businessman and he didn't dump me. He got married!

Her drunken indignation dissolves into helpless tears.

He got married!

GUY (*soothingly, trying to steer her into the building*). He's Italian, Sweetie. They always get married.

DELIA *emerges from her bedroom in robe and slippers and comes outside to see what all the noise is about.* LELAND *is still hovering awkwardly around the stoop.* ANGEL *is now weeping and clinging to* GUY.

DELIA. What happened?

She takes ANGEL'*s other arm.*

GUY. Nick got married.

ANGEL (*wailing*). Don't keep saying it!

GUY. Sh-h-h! It's okay. Come on now. Here we go.

As DELIA, GUY *and* ANGEL *go inside Guy's apartment,* LELAND *stands looking after them. He turns to go and sees that* ANGEL *has dropped the chiffon scarf she had draped around her neck. His first impulse is to return it immediately, but then he stops, folds it carefully and puts it in his breast pocket, then exits.*

Upstairs, GUY *is making coffee on the hot plate.* DELIA *is taking off* ANGEL*'s shoes and jewelry, and is putting one of Guy's robes on her.* ANGEL *is drunk and miserable.*

ANGEL. He left me, Deal! He left me!

DELIA. He didn't deserve you.

ANGEL. But I loved him.

DELIA. Of course you did.

GUY. Hang on, Sweetie. Coffee coming up!

ANGEL. I don't want coffee! I want champagne! We're celebrating! Aren't we celebrating?

DELIA. Come on now. Let me help you… Just relax, okay?

ANGEL. Relax? How can I relax? I just got fired! I got fired, Deal!

DELIA. Fired? She got fired? You didn't tell me she got fired.

GUY. The night is young. The whole sordid story has just begun to unfold.

ANGEL. I thought when he came backstage to tell me he was married, he'd go on home to his wife and leave me in peace to do the show. He must have known my heart was broken, but when we came out to do 'Wild About Harry,' he was sitting right in the front in his regular seat with Frankie and that other scary guy and they were toasting him and celebrating… They were having a party right up in my face! What could I do?

GUY (*bringing coffee*). Next time ask me that before you go onstage.

ANGEL. I hate coffee. Put some brandy in it.

GUY. Drink it!

DELIA. What did she do?

GUY. When they got to the part where they say, 'The heavenly blisses of his kisses fill me with ecstasy,' Miss Angel broke out of the line, walked over to his table and told Nick all about his sorry self.

DELIA. From the stage?

GUY. Centerstage, thank you. She read his titles clear for about two minutes, then she burst into tears and the stage manager came and took her away. He threw her and her stuff out into the middle of Lenox Avenue. We've been 'celebrating' ever since.

DELIA. They can't fire her for that, can they?

GUY. For cussing out a short-tempered gangster in the middle of an up-tempo production number?

ANGEL. I didn't curse him. I couldn't curse Nicky. I love him.

GUY. Okay, Sweetie. Time for bed before we start back down that road.

ANGEL. I don't want to go to bed. What kind of dreams am I gonna have, huh? No man. No job.

GUY. There are still plenty of clubs in Harlem looking for a fine woman who can sing.

ANGEL. I can't sing anymore. My heart is broken.

GUY. You can sing the blues.

ANGEL. Everybody in Harlem is singing the blues.

GUY. Then you can come to Paris with me. Give Josephine some competition.

GUY *covers* ANGEL *with a blanket. She snuggles down like a child and draws the covers up to her chin. She is fading fast.*

ANGEL. Are we really going to Paris, Big Daddy?

GUY. Oui, ma chérie. We are really and truly going. Any day now.

ANGEL. What's the boat going to be like?

GUY. A ship. Not a boat. It's too elegant to be a boat.

ANGEL. And are we elegant too?

GUY. We are très, très élégant!

ANGEL. You gonna save me again, Big Daddy?

GUY. Every chance I get.

> GUY *kisses* ANGEL's *cheek.* GUY *and* DELIA *talk quietly, but* ANGEL *is already sleeping.*

> Sorry we woke you up. Want some champagne?

> *He takes out a bottle and two glasses.*

DELIA. It's three o'clock in the morning!

GUY. You are going to have to get over this primitive idea you have that the world shuts down between ten p.m. and seven a.m.

> *He hands her a glass.*

> Cheers!

DELIA. Do you think she really loved Nicky?

GUY. I don't think that was part of their deal.

DELIA (*looking thoughtfully at the sleeping* ANGEL). Maybe I can teach her how to type.

GUY. Teach who how to type?

DELIA. Angel. I've got this typing correspondence course.

GUY. You don't have a typewriter.

DELIA. They sent a folding chart so I can practice until I get one.

GUY. What makes you think Angel wants to learn how to type?

DELIA. I think she's scared she won't be able to find another singing job.

GUY. She better be scared. Half the singers in Harlem are looking for work.

DELIA. You just said there were plenty of places…

GUY. She already got dumped and fired. I figured that was enough bad news for one Saturday night.

DELIA. Well, thanks for the champagne. I'm going back to bed. Church in the morning.

GUY. Adam Powell must be preaching.

DELIA (*blushing guiltily*). As a matter of fact, he is.

GUY. You all need to leave that poor man alone. Finish your champagne.

DELIA. I want to tell him about the clinic. You should come go with me. Help me get my nerve up.

GUY. You've got nerve to spare already. Besides, young Reverend Powell is not my type, thank you. The truth of the matter is, the finest young thing I've seen in ages walked home with me and Angel.

DELIA. The man with you downstairs? Was he a friend of yours?

GUY. Never saw him before in my life. He saw me struggling down 125th Street with a drunken woman in my arms and took pity on us.

DELIA. A friend of Angel's?

GUY. He's a stranger is what I'm trying to tell you. A mysterious gentleman who came to our aid and then melted back into the Harlem night.

DELIA. That's very romantic.

GUY. I thought so. That's one of the secrets of life, Young Miss. Don't forget it. Learn to spot the romance. For example...

He presents a new costume sketch with a flourish.

Voilà!

DELIA. It's wonderful! When did you...?

GUY. Last night. I dreamed it. I saw Josephine walking down the center staircase of one of those fabulous Folies Bergère sets in this very dress. And feel this.

*He gently hands her a carefully folded piece of brilliant
magenta satin.*

Satin. Isn't it wonderful?

DELIA (*awed by the richness of the fabric*). Can you imagine
sleeping on satin sheets?

GUY. I understand your pastor is partial to them.

DELIA. Who told you that?

GUY. I run in international circles, girl. I have my sources.
Look at you! I don't know how you can traipse around
Harlem all day talking about opening birth-control clinics
and then blush when I tell you your pastor sleeps on satin
sheets.

DELIA. I just never thought about it.

GUY (*suddenly*). Deal, can I ask you something personal?

DELIA. What if I say no?

GUY. I'll ask you anyway.

DELIA. Then go ahead.

GUY. Are you a virgin?

DELIA (*flustered and indignant; she clearly is*). I'm twenty-five
years old!

GUY. That's what I thought! How wonderful! To be present at
the awakening of another young fawn!

DELIA. What makes you think I'm awakening?

GUY. You're already drinking French champagne with a
notorious homosexual at three o'clock on Sunday morning!
What more proof do you need?

DELIA. Just don't tell Angel. She already treats me like I'm her
little sister.

GUY. She treats everybody like they're her little sister. Drink up!

*He pours more champagne and raises his glass to the
photograph of Josephine Baker.*

To Josephine. Paris has never seen costumes like the ones
I'm designing for La Bakaire!

DELIA. Do you ever think you won't go?

GUY. I'm going. Besides I have no choice. The matter is now
officially out of my hands. Angel wasn't the only one who
got fired last evening.

DELIA. You? Why?

GUY. Well, I couldn't hardly stand by and let Bobby toss her
bodily out into the street, could I?

DELIA. What are you going to do?

GUY. I'm going to drive Josephine crazy until she sends for me.
She promised she would and I'm going to take her at her
word.

DELIA. I've got a little money saved if you need anything.

GUY. Aren't you sweet?

He kisses her.

I'm fine for now. I've got a couple of jobs working on the
outside, thank God! Do me a favor?

DELIA. Sure.

GUY. Don't tell Angel. I don't want her to panic. I can take care
of both of us if I have to. It won't be the first time.

DELIA. I promise.

GUY. Thanks.

DELIA *looks at* ANGEL *sleeping soundly.*

DELIA. Maybe I'll bring that typing chart by after church
anyway. She might want to… try something new.

GUY. Forget the charts. Come by after service and finish this
champagne with us.

DELIA. Does it have to be either-or?

GUY. Everything is either-or, Sweetie. Goodnight.

DELIA. Goodnight. (*A beat.*) Do you really think I have nerve to spare?

GUY. No question.

He kisses her cheek. DELIA *crosses the hall to her own apartment, removes her shoes and robe and gets back into bed.* GUY *closes his door. He walks quietly over to check on* ANGEL *and fixes her covers gently as the lights go to black.*

Scene Two

Later that afternoon. Guy's apartment is quiet. ANGEL *is still curled up on the sofa.* GUY *enters carrying a small overnight bag and comes upstairs. He opens the door to his apartment and sees no signs of life. He sets the bag down and peers at* ANGEL, *then goes over and shakes her gently. No activity. He removes his coat and hat, puts on coffee and shakes her again. She groans.*

ANGEL. Go away!

GUY. Rise and shine!

ANGEL. Are you crazy? What time is it?

GUY. Half-past noon, Sweetie.

ANGEL. Are you kidding? God! I feel like hell.

GUY. You look pretty bad, too.

ANGEL. Thanks. What have we got to drink?

GUY. Coffee.

She glares at him.

But since you asked so nicely, I'll put some brandy in it for you.

ANGEL. Aspirin?

GUY. We're out. Again.

ANGEL. Where were we last night anyway?

GUY. Don't you remember?

ANGEL. If I remembered I wouldn't be – oh!

GUY. I thought it might come back to you.

ANGEL. Did I – ?

GUY. You did.

ANGEL. Did they – ?

GUY. They did.

ANGEL. Fired me?

GUY. Like you stole something.

ANGEL. They'll take me back though, won't they? I mean, if I go down and talk nice to Bobby, he'll understand. I didn't throw anything, did I?

A beat. He looks at her. Clearly, she did.

GUY. Drink your coffee before you get yourself all worked up.

ANGEL *drinks the coffee slowly.*

ANGEL. Do you think they'll take me back? Really, I mean.

GUY. Truth or solace?

ANGEL. Truth.

GUY. Not a chance.

ANGEL. What the hell am I gonna do now?

GUY. We'll think of something.

ANGEL. Like what? The Depression has killed all the nightlife in Harlem and nobody's gonna hire me downtown after what I said to Nick.

GUY. You can always come to Paris with me.

ANGEL. Sure I can.

GUY. I'm serious.

ANGEL. I know you are, but you being serious doesn't pay the rent.

GUY. Which brings us to my last little piece of good news.

ANGEL. I can hardly wait.

GUY. I went by your place.

ANGEL. This morning?

GUY. I figured Nicky's Catholic, he should be in church on Sunday morning...

ANGEL. With his wife.

GUY. ...so that might be a good time to go get your stuff with a minimum of confusion.

ANGEL. What kind of confusion?

GUY. I don't think the details are particularly important except to say that the doorman let me go up for a fast five minutes to get what I convinced him were irreplaceable and exotic medicines which you had to have or die an agonizing and immediate death which would be on his conscience forever, especially if you expired on the Sabbath.

He hands her the small bag.

I grabbed what I could.

ANGEL. This is it?

GUY. I only had five minutes, Sweetie.

ANGEL. He told me I could stay there as long as I wanted to. Think of it as your place, that's what he told me!

GUY. Think of it as your old place. And welcome to your new one.

ANGEL. I can't stay here. You know last time we tried that we stopped speaking to each other for a month.

GUY. Okay.

He waits.

ANGEL (*quietly*). Go to hell.

GUY. Don't worry about it. It'll be just like old times. Tripping over your stuff on the way to the toilet. Worrying about you wearing all my good clothes. You're over here half the time anyway. What's the big deal?

ANGEL. Guy…

She looks at him without speaking. He sees/senses her fear. They have had this kind of conversation many times before.

GUY. Look, even in your current sorry state, you're better off than most of the Negroes in Harlem. You've got a place to stay and I'm not gonna let you starve to death. We'll figure it out.

ANGEL. I should be figuring things out for myself.

GUY. Shoulda, coulda, woulda.

ANGEL. My head hurts too bad to argue.

GUY. Have I ever let you down?

ANGEL. You know you haven't.

GUY. I know I haven't, but I'm asking you.

A beat. He waits.

ANGEL. No, you have never let me down.

GUY. You think I'm gonna start now?

ANGEL. No, I don't think you're gonna start now.

GUY. Then stop worrying and pull yourself together. Big Daddy's gonna keep everything fine and mellow. Just like always.

ANGEL. But I'm so broke. I owe everybody…

GUY. Just… like… always. Okay?

ANGEL. I love you.

GUY. I love you too, Sweetie.

DELIA *enters from church and knocks loudly on their door.*
ANGEL *groans and falls back, holding her head.* DELIA
pokes her head in.

DELIA. How is she?

GUY. She's alive.

DELIA. How are you feeling?

ANGEL. How do I look?

DELIA. Well...

ANGEL. Never mind. Do you have any aspirin?

DELIA. I think I've got some across the hall. I've got something
else to show you, too, but I'll wait until you're feeling better.

DELIA *winks conspiratorially at* GUY *and goes to get the
aspirin. During the dialogue that follows,* DELIA *looks
around for aspirin, but finds none. On her way out, she picks
up the typing chart and book and takes them back across the
hall with her.*

ANGEL. I can hardly wait. What is she talking about?

GUY. She wants to teach you how to use a typewriter.

ANGEL. What?

Throughout this scene, GUY *works at his sewing while
participating fully in the conversation. This is his habit, and
his friends are all used to it.*

GUY. Since you said you couldn't sing anymore because of your
broken heart, Deal thought you might want to take advantage
of the growing opportunities in the secretarial pool.

ANGEL. Tell me it hasn't come to that.

GUY. It hasn't come to that.

ANGEL. Swear it.

GUY. I swear it.

ANGEL. My head is killing me. Where is that child with the
aspirin?

GUY. Sam's coming by this afternoon. He'll have some.

ANGEL. When did you see Sam?

GUY. We saw him. Last night at Small's.

ANGEL. God! I don't even remember being at Small's. Was I already drunk?

GUY. Let's just say, the question was already beside the point.

ANGEL (*remembering vaguely*). Did he walk home with us?

GUY. No. We left him at the club. He delivered five babies yesterday. He was celebrating their arrival.

ANGEL. I thought there was somebody else...

GUY. A brother walked with us part of the way from 125th Street. Saw a damsel in distress and offered his assistance. A real Southern gentleman from the accent. Beautiful silk suit, too.

ANGEL. A silk suit? I thought you said he was Southern.

GUY. I didn't say Southern bumpkin.

ANGEL. Who was he?

GUY. I never saw him around before.

ANGEL. Didn't you ask him?

GUY. I was a little preoccupied.

    DELIA *returns to the apartment.*

DELIA. I'm sorry. I guess I'm out too.

    ANGEL *groans.*

ANGEL. Well, let's pray for Sam.

    She lies down and closes her eyes.

DELIA. Is Sam coming?

GUY. Any minute now.

DELIA. Oh, well. I'll go on then.

GUY. Why? Doc's family.

DELIA. He's just so...

GUY. What?

DELIA. Sometimes he doesn't seem like a doctor. He's out as much as you and Angel.

GUY. Are we now the standard of dissipation?

DELIA. No, but he's a doctor.

GUY. Doctors can't like jazz?

DELIA. It's not the music. It's the way he acts. Whoever heard of a doctor going around hollering...

GUY. 'Let the good times roll!' And he doesn't holler. He speaks with conviction.

DELIA. Does that sound like a serious physician to you?

GUY. Relax, Sweetie. Sam's the best doctor in New York City. He'll work his magic on Angel and we'll all go out to eat.

ANGEL. Don't talk about food!

DELIA. Angel?

No response.

Can I show you something?

ANGEL. No!

DELIA. Oh, well.

A beat. She decides to plow ahead anyway. She lies out the typing chart and book.

I can just leave it for you, then. You can look at it later. Whenever you feel like it. I don't need it back right away or anything. (*A beat.*) I just thought maybe you... last night... you sounded like... you might want to try something new... and there are expanding opportunities in the secretarial pool.

ANGEL *groans loudly.*

GUY. Your timing is lousy, Deal. Come tell me what the good Reverend Powell was up to this morning.

DELIA. He was wonderful! He got so worked up at the end of his sermon, he came out of the pulpit, walked straight down the middle aisle and right up Seventh Avenue. His robe was billowing out around him like wings...

GUY. That Negro ought to quit preaching and go on into full-time show business.

DELIA. By the time he turned around and came back he had picked up twenty new members and the choir was still singing the invitational hymn. And guess what else?

GUY. A dove landed on his shoulder and a voice said...

DELIA. I talked to him about the clinic.

GUY. You did?

DELIA. And I wasn't even nervous. I was in line to shake his hand after service and he said he was happy to see I had decided to make Abyssinian my church home. And I said I was proud to be a part of a church that had a sense of responsibility to the masses.

GUY. Not those Negroes again.

DELIA (*a little defensive*). He knew what I meant! The people of Harlem. The women who need...

ANGEL *groans*.

ANGEL. Please don't get her all worked up! I can't take the history of the downtrodden without some aspirin!

GUY. Our apologies, Madam. We forgot the presence of the infirm in our midst. (*To* DELIA.) Go on.

DELIA. So then I said I was working with Margaret Sanger to open a family planning clinic right here in Harlem.

GUY. You said 'family planning' in the fellowship line at Abyssinian? (*Laughs*.) I hope none of those high-tones from Sugar Hill heard you.

DELIA. Then Reverend Powell said it sounded like a very interesting idea and to come by the church office on Monday so I could tell him more about it.

GUY. Well, all-reet! You hear that, Angel?

ANGEL (*groaning*). I want Sam!

> SAM *enters from the street and comes in their open door.*

SAM. Ask and ye shall receive! It's a boy!

GUY. My favorite Harlem healer! Come on in, Doc.

DELIA. How's the mother?

SAM. You didn't let me finish. It's also a girl.

DELIA. Twins?

SAM. Mother and babies are doing fine.

ANGEL. Just what Harlem needs. Two more mouths to feed.

GUY. Don't listen to the cynic. Congratulations!

SAM. Thank you on behalf of all concerned. Especially the
proud father who also happens to be a successful bootlegger.

> *He pulls a bottle from his coat pocket.*

GUY (*going to get glasses or cups for everybody*). I'm liking
this family more all the time.

SAM (*to* ANGEL). How're you feeling?

ANGEL. Tell me you have aspirin or shoot me.

SAM. Here, try this.

> *He hands her some pills from his pocket.*

ANGEL. What is it?

SAM. Just aspirin. Hospital-strength. I've found it to be very
effective in treating the Harlem hangover.

> *He hands her a glass of the bootleg liquor, and she swallows
> it with the pills.*

DELIA (*as* SAM *pours for the others*). Is it really safe for us to
drink it?

GUY. Just enough to toast the new arrivals.

DELIA. Aren't you afraid we'll go blind or something?

SAM. Don't worry. I'm a doctor.

He holds up his glass.

To the two newest citizens of Harlem! Long life, good
health, and let the good times roll!

GUY. Amen!

They all drink.

SAM. Feeling anything yet?

ANGEL. Not yet.

SAM. It just takes a minute. I promise.

He drains his glass.

Seven babies in two days. I think it's a record. Even for me!

GUY. Then you deserve another drink.

SAM. Thank you, kind sir.

Pouring another for himself and for GUY.

You know, that woman almost didn't make it.

DELIA. The mother?

SAM. They didn't even know she was carrying twins and one
of them was coming breech. When I let her husband know
what the risks were, he broke down and cried. He kept
saying, 'That's the best woman in the world in there, Doc.
That's the best woman in the world.'

DELIA. If she's so precious to him, why didn't he take her to
the doctor?

SAM. He did. He just took her a little late, that's all.

GUY. Why didn't she take herself? If she's old enough to have
two babies at one time, she ought to be able to figure out
how to catch the subway.

ANGEL (*suddenly*). It worked!

SAM. I told you.

ANGEL. It's a miracle! You're a genius, Sam! They ought to put you in charge of Harlem Hospital.

SAM. That's not my reward, is it?

GUY. No. Your reward is you get to take us all out for Sunday dinner. Can you come, Deal?

DELIA. Well, I…

SAM (*interrupting her quickly before she can refuse*). Great idea! What do you think, Angel? Ready for solid food yet?

ANGEL. Not a chance. You all go on though. I'll be fine.

DELIA. Want us to bring you back a plate?

GUY. If you think I'm going to join the Sunday promenade carrying a plate of leftover collard greens, you could not be more wrong!

SAM. Let's go. Now that you said 'food,' I'm starving!

DELIA. Give me five minutes.

GUY. Take ten. I need to freshen up myself.

SAM. Good. I'll take a quick nap.

   DELIA *exits to her apartment,* GUY *to the bedroom.* SAM *sits slumped in his chair with his eyes closed.* ANGEL *watches him. He speaks without opening his eyes.*

   So how is it, Angel Eyes?

ANGEL. It's been better.

SAM. Well, look on the bright side.

ANGEL. What bright side is that?

SAM. I met a bootlegger and found a cure for hangover in the same week.

ANGEL. Nice work if you can get it.

   ANGEL *is pacing around restlessly.* SAM *opens his eyes and watches her.*

SAM. Why don't you sing me some Sunday morning blues?

ANGEL. Didn't your mama teach you not to sing no blues on the Lord's day?

SAM *leans back and closes his eyes again wearily.*

SAM. My mama taught me that man was the beginning and end of his own misery and that calling on God to fix it once you broke it was a comfort we were not allowed.

ANGEL (*sitting beside him and stroking his forehead maternally*). Your mama said a mouthful to answer a simple question, huh?

SAM. The curse of the Negro intellectual.

A beat.

ANGEL. You look like hell.

SAM (*eyes still closed*). The pot calling the kettle…

ANGEL. But you're supposed to be respectable.

SAM. Our recent population explosion didn't leave me much time to get my suit pressed. I don't look that bad, do I?

ANGEL. Terrible. You need somebody to take care of you, Doc. I'm looking for a job. Let's get married.

SAM. Wait 'til I tell you what my mother said about marriage.

ANGEL. Too bad. I'd be a great wife. You'd come home from a hard day's work, and I'd be there with a hot, home-cooked meal on the table and your slippers by the fire.

SAM. Can't you be there in a red satin shimmy singing 'St Louis Blues' and drinking bathtub gin?

ANGEL. That's not the wife! That's the girlfriend.

SAM. Okay. Lose the shimmy. Lose the gin. Keep the blues.

A beat.

ANGEL. Why didn't we ever get together?

SAM. Because you deserve better.

A beat. She is moved by the directness of his response, but then she laughs as if he was only teasing.

ANGEL. All right, smooth talker! If I go to hell, it's on your conscience.

She begins to sing a song like 'St Louis Blues' by W.C. Handy.

DELIA *re-enters.* ANGEL *sings her way over to* DELIA *and begins dancing with her as she sings.* DELIA *is shy, but delighted.* SAM *watches them affectionately.*

SAM. I didn't realize your revolution left a space for dancing.

ANGEL (*still dancing*). All revolutions leave a space for dancing. They just like to pretend they don't.

DELIA *stops dancing.*

DELIA (*defensive*). I'm not trying to make a revolution. I'm just trying to give women in Harlem the chance to plan their families.

SAM. From what I hear, your Mrs Sanger said that's where the whole thing begins. Women's bodies out of their control. Sickly kids and sorry men everywhere you look.

DELIA *is becoming more agitated. She doesn't know* SAM *well and she's never sure when he is teasing her.*

And she's right, of course!

He raises a glass, still teasing.

Here's to victory for your side.

GUY (*re-enters dressed to go out*). I leave for five minutes and you all are choosing up sides. What did you do, Angel?

ANGEL. Me? I didn't do anything. I sang 'St Louis Blues' for Doc and...

GUY. Well, there you go. What did your mama tell you about singing those low-down blues on Sunday morning?

ANGEL (*to* SAM). I warned you!

GUY. Change your mind and come with us.

ANGEL. Where are you going?

GUY. Probably down to Ike Hines's.

ANGEL. Chinese food?

SAM. I have the feeling Delia's changing her mind about going anywhere with me.

DELIA. It's just not funny to me, that's all. Women are dying…

GUY. Don't pay Sam any mind. He can't help it. (*To* ANGEL.) Coming?

ANGEL. It's too early in the day for chop suey.

GUY. Well, try to behave yourself until we get back. Everybody ready?

SAM (*to* DELIA). It's not funny to me either. I apologize. I was just teasing because I didn't know how to tell the two of you how beautiful you looked dancing in the sunlight. It won't happen again.

SAM extends his arm and, after a slight hesitation, DELIA takes it.

GUY. Well, la-di-dah! Now can we eat?

DELIA. I'm starving.

The rest of the conversation takes place as they exit.

Do you want to go by the reading at the Y afterward?

GUY. Not unless Langston is going to be there.

SAM. Langston's not back yet, is he?

GUY. There's your answer!

They exit. ANGEL *watches them go from the window. She walks absentmindedly around the apartment. She looks at the typing chart and open typing book. She holds her hands over the chart as if preparing to type, then shudders and moves away. She picks up a fan and fans herself languidly. When she passes the window, she leans out, still fanning, hoping for something to catch her eye.*

LELAND *enters. He is well dressed in a dark suit, white shirt and tie. She sees him as he sees her, but she does not remember him from last night. He looks at her without embarrassment. She smiles at him, intrigued, fanning seductively.*

ANGEL. Hot enough for you?

LELAND. Yes, ma'am.

ANGEL (*amused by his formality*). You're not from around here, huh?

LELAND. I'm from Alabama.

ANGEL. You a long way from home, Alabama.

LELAND. My name is Leland.

ANGEL. First or last?

LELAND. I beg your pardon?

ANGEL. Leland your first name or your last one?

LELAND. First one. Leland Cunningham's my full Christian name.

ANGEL. And are you a Christian, Mr Leland Cunningham?

LELAND. I try to be.

ANGEL. Good for you. (*A beat.*) I'm Angel. You looking for somebody, or you just looking?

LELAND. I was looking for you.

ANGEL. I think you've got me confused with somebody else.

LELAND. Last night. (*A beat.*) With your... friend. He was taking you home and I...

ANGEL. You're not my Southern gentleman, are you?

LELAND. I guess I am...

ANGEL. Well, thank you for your assistance. (*A beat.*) But what are you doing here today?

LELAND. I just wanted to see if you were feeling all right.

ANGEL. I'm feeling fine. Just fine... thanks.

LELAND. Well, good. I just wanted to be sure everything was... that you were okay.

A beat. She watches him, fanning herself slowly.

ANGEL. So how hot does it get in Alabama?

LELAND. It's pretty near always this hot down there. One way or another.

ANGEL. Well, it's not always this hot in Harlem, but today it is. (*A beat.*) Do you know what I mean?

LELAND. I'm not sure that I do.

ANGEL. What I mean is, it's a little too hot today for a lady to take a stroll with a gentleman friend even if the idea presented itself to her.

He looks at her. A beat. He wants this to be the right answer.

LELAND. It's supposed to be a lot cooler by the weekend.

ANGEL. You keep up with the weather, do you?

LELAND. I grew up on a farm. Old habits are hard to break.

ANGEL. All right, Alabama, why don't you come by next Sunday evening and we'll take us an old-fashioned Southern stroll.

LELAND. Around seven?

ANGEL. Apartment Two.

LELAND. I won't be late.

ANGEL. I know you won't, Alabama. It's not in your nature.

LELAND. Call me Leland.

ANGEL. Leland.

He tips his hat and exits. She smiles after him as the lights go to black.

Scene Three

Wednesday, late afternoon. DELIA *is unwrapping a box that has arrived in the mail. On top of the tissue paper inside is a note in a small envelope.* DELIA *reads the note, smiles and puts it aside. She folds back the tissue paper and pulls out a dress. It is a bright color and very different from the plain suits* DELIA *usually wears. She looks at it, holds it up against herself and smiles. She even twirls a little, imagining herself in the dress. She lays it carefully aside and returns to the table where she was working earlier. She picks up her pen and begins to work. She stops suddenly, looks up at the dress, smiles again and then focuses completely on her work.*

ANGEL *enters downstairs and walks slowly up the stairs. She kicks off her shoes and drops her hat as soon as she enters the apartment. Guy is not home, and the apartment is empty. She is wearing a fairly dressy suit. She sighs and then begins looking around for something. She looks under cushions, chairs and in drawers. Not finding what she is looking for, she stops in frustration, looks around the room. She thinks hard as she looks at the sewing corner, listens, looks out the window to see who might be coming. Seeing no one, she moves swiftly to the sewing area, opens a drawer; nothing. She listens again. Opens another drawer. Victory! She holds up a bottle of liquor with guilty relief. She grabs a glass, pours a shot and gulps it, eyes closed. She relaxes a little, then pours another drink. Carefully, she puts the bottle back. She sits down and holds the drink close to her.* GUY *enters downstairs. She hears him on the steps, gulps down her drink and puts the glass under the chair.*

GUY *enters with several bolts of fabric. He is pleased to see* ANGEL, *who stands guiltily, holding her hat.*

GUY. Well, hey, Sweetie!

He kisses her on both cheeks.

Comment ça va? You just walk in the door?

ANGEL. Just this minute. Where've you been?

GUY. Over at the Hole in the Wall measuring these chubby little chorus girls who keep trying to lie about their weight when I'm sitting right there with a tape measure.

ANGEL. Why are you working at that dive? What's Bobby gonna say?

GUY. The money was too good to turn it down. I sound like a whore, don't I?

ANGEL. Not yet.

GUY. Thanks for the vote of confidence. And how was your day?

ANGEL. Terrible, thanks.

GUY. No luck, huh?

ANGEL. There are no singing jobs in Harlem. Period.

GUY. Well, it's not too late to take Deal up on her offer to teach you typing.

ANGEL. That isn't funny. I've been all over Harlem and nobody will even give me the time of day. There aren't any jobs doing anything, especially singing for your supper. Whole families sitting on the sidewalk with their stuff set out beside them. No place to sleep. No place to wash. Walking all day.

GUY. Listen, Sweetie… I saw Nick.

ANGEL. You spoke to him?

GUY. He asked me where you were working and I had to confess you were between engagements.

ANGEL. It's all his fault, the sorry bastard.

GUY. He said he felt bad about what had happened and he gave me a number for you to call about an audition. A club downtown.

ANGEL. Really? Which one?

GUY. Here.

GUY *pulls a piece of paper from his pocket and hands it to* ANGEL. *She reads it, face falls for a minute, then she regroups and looks on the bright side.*

ANGEL. I know this guy. He's a friend of Nick's. You know Tony T.

GUY. I've seen him around...

ANGEL. Why'd you say it like that?

GUY. I just don't think he's looking for a singer.

A beat. She looks stunned.

ANGEL. Nick wouldn't do that.

GUY *is silent.*

He said an audition, right?

A beat.

GUY. You can't make it real just because you want it to be.

ANGEL. Are you really going to Paris?

GUY. It's not the same thing.

ANGEL. Why isn't it? Because you're some kind of genius with a dream and I'm just a colored woman out of a job?

GUY. Is that your dream? Singing for gangsters? And then what?

ANGEL. Then I'll have to figure out something else. Isn't that what you always tell me? 'One step at a time.'

GUY. Okay. One step at a time. Audition. Sing your heart out and if he acts a fool, me and Sam will cut his heart out for him.

ANGEL. It's a deal.

GUY. Just don't ask me to make you anything to wear. I don't have time and I can't make time. You're on your own.

ANGEL. You can make twelve outfits for those Hole in the Wall floozies and not one little dress for me?

GUY. They're not floozies and their boss is paying enough to get me halfway to Paris.

ANGEL. How long can it take to run up one little dress?

GUY. Wear your suit. It still looks great on you.

ANGEL. Everybody's already seen it!

GUY. You're not going to let me say no, are you?

ANGEL. Not if I can help it.

GUY. I'll alter the suit… slightly! And I'll make you a hat. That's my final offer.

ANGEL. I swear I will never ask you for anything again!

GUY. Let's have a drink before you make any more promises you can't possibly keep.

ANGEL (*innocently*). Do we have anything? I thought we drank the last of that.

He goes to the bottle ANGEL *has recently restashed. He squints at the level of the alcohol.*

GUY. Well, we didn't, but we're working on it.

He pours two drinks and hands one to ANGEL.

ANGEL. You know everywhere I went this week there were twenty people in line ahead of me. I've never seen things this bad all over. Nobody's working and nobody's got prospects.

GUY. For prospects, you gotta look past 125th Street. No law says we gotta live and die in Harlem, USA, just 'cause we happened to wind up here when we finally blew out of Savannah. The world is a big place!

ANGEL. Getting smaller every day.

GUY. No it isn't. I can look out of this very window and see us walking arm in arm down the Champs Élysées.

ANGEL. Remember how you used to take those old broke-up binoculars whenever we'd go to the beach at home? The only Negro in the world ever tried to see Paris from the coast of Georgia.

GUY. I am not! Langston said he used to… oh, my God! I almost forgot! He's back!

ANGEL. Langston? Since when?

GUY. Since last Saturday. I ran into Bruce Nugent and he said the group is gathering at his place later for a welcome home. Everybody is going to be there. Want to go preen?

ANGEL. Can I wear your tux?

GUY. I'm wearing my tux! Why don't you go very femme? You'll probably be the only lady at this affair. Show them what they're missing.

ANGEL. I hate being the only girl. You always abandon me the first time some sweet young thing flutters his eyelashes at you, then I'm stuck the rest of the night making small talk with guys who are still pretending not to know why they came there.

GUY. Okay. Let's take Deal.

ANGEL (*laughing*). Deal's not ready for one of Bruce's parties and you know it.

GUY. Well, it's time she got ready. Go ask her. We all deserve a night out!

ANGEL. I can return her chart, too, thank God!

GUY. I'm going to take a quick nap since Bruce's parties require one to be both ravishing and alert. Wake me at seven if you don't hear me up, will you? Dinner's at eight.

ANGEL. Dinner? How rich is Bruce's new lover?

GUY. It's just buffet, darling. He may have long money but he's not going to try and feed the entire Negro demimonde!

ANGEL. I'll wake you in plenty of time.

She crosses the hall to knock at Delia's apartment door. GUY goes into the bedroom for his nap. DELIA is working. She answers the door reluctantly.

Are you busy?

DELIA. Well, I'm working on some stuff for Reverend Powell.

ANGEL. But don't you want to hear the news?

DELIA *pauses*.

It's good news.

DELIA. All right.

ANGEL. I'm not going to learn how to type.

She hands the chart back to DELIA.

Want to know why?

DELIA. Why?

ANGEL. I got an audition!

DELIA. That's wonderful! Where?

ANGEL. A place downtown. The owner's a friend of Nick's. He's always wanted me to sing there so I think the audition is pretty much just for show.

DELIA. You should do that song you were singing on Sunday.

ANGEL. Those Italians don't care nothin' about no blues. They like hotsy-totsy girls, grinnin' and shakin' and singin' all at the same damn time. (*A beat*.) Can I tell you something?

DELIA. Sure…

ANGEL. Guy got fired.

DELIA. How do you know?

ANGEL. I went to the club today to beg Bobby for my job back.

DELIA. What did he say?

ANGEL. They fired him the same night they did me!

DELIA. I mean about your old job.

ANGEL. Not a chance. Of course, he let me beg for a while before he said no. (*A beat*.) I couldn't figure out why Guy was taking work from dives like the Hole in the Wall, but he hasn't got any choice.

DELIA. He says it won't be for long. Just until…

ANGEL. Don't say it! The myth of the magical Josephine. She practically lives with us but so far I haven't seen her share of the rent money!

DELIA. Guy says he expects to hear from her by the end of the month.

ANGEL. Guy says, Guy says! He's been sending her sketches for a year but have you seen a return cable? A letter? A postcard of the Eiffel Tower? Nothing! Nothing but that damn picture hanging up there grinning at me all day and all night! (*A beat*.) Guy's a dreamer. He always was and he always will be, but I'm gonna hitch my star to somebody a little closer to home. (*Suddenly brightens*.) I almost forgot the rest of my good news! Langston's back and you have to come with us to the welcome home party!

DELIA. I don't even know Langston Hughes.

ANGEL. Half the people there don't know him either. That's what makes it fun. To see the ones who don't try to pretend to be the ones who do.

DELIA. I can't tonight. Sam's coming over.

ANGEL. Sam's coming here? When?

DELIA. In a little while. Reverend Powell suggested I ask him to help me get ready for the deacon's meeting next week. Some of them aren't crazy about the clinic. (*A beat*.) I didn't even know Reverend Powell knew Sam.

ANGEL. Everybody knows Sam, this is just his first time calling on you.

DELIA. He's not calling on me. We're working together.

ANGEL. He thinks you're adorable.

DELIA. What are you talking about?

ANGEL. You don't think he was grinning at me dancing in the sunshine, do you?

DELIA. Then why is he always teasing me?

ANGEL. It's just his way. (*Notices the new dress*.) Deal... you don't have anything I can wear, do you? For the audition? I've worn this to death and I lost all my other stuff at Nicky's.

DELIA. I don't think so. Most of my stuff is... plain.

ANGEL. I know!

DELIA. Social workers are supposed to blend in, otherwise we scare people.

ANGEL. Those suits they make you wear are what scare people. I begged Guy to make me something new, but he's crazy trying to get Josephine's things done and these new costumes for... (*As if she just noticed the dress*.) Deal! What about this? Is it new?

DELIA. My aunt just sent it to me. She doesn't like my suits much either.

ANGEL. It's beautiful. Do you think it would fit me? I know we're not exactly the same size, but I think I could... can I try it?

DELIA. Well, I guess so.

ANGEL stops suddenly.

ANGEL. What is wrong with me? This is a brand-new dress, isn't it? You're probably saving it for something special.

DELIA. An audition is something special, isn't it?

ANGEL. Thanks, Deal. Really.

She puts on the dress immediately.

Zip me up!

The dress looks great.

How do I look?

DELIA. Better than I ever will in it!

ANGEL. It's perfect! I can't lose! I'll be a big star in no time and we'll both go to Paris and drink champagne and marry two rich old Frenchmen who will die immediately and leave us everything!

DELIA. Sounds wonderful, but I've got to get back to work.

A beat.

ANGEL. Look at you, Deal. You got bags under your eyes like an old woman. All tired and frowned up.

DELIA. I do look tired, don't I?

ANGEL. Sit down here for a minute. Can I take your hair aloose?

DELIA. Angel…

ANGEL. This will only take a minute, I promise.

DELIA *sits, and* ANGEL *begins to massage her head expertly. As* ANGEL *talks, we see* DELIA*'s body relax.*

A New Orleans Voodoo woman showed me how to do this when I was a little girl back in Savannah.

DELIA. What was she doing in Savannah?

ANGEL. The Voodoo woman? What does anybody do anywhere? How does that feel?

DELIA. Wonderful.

ANGEL. You have to use your whole hand. All the fingers at the same time, but not too hard. Just enough.

DELIA (*her eyes closed*). It feels like everything is just… floating away.

ANGEL (*massaging* DELIA*'s head expertly and gently as she speaks*). When I was working at Miss Lillie's, as many of those old men would pay me for this as would pay me for the other.

DELIA. I don't know how you can talk about it like that.

ANGEL. Talk about what like that?

DELIA. About what happened to you.

ANGEL. It was better than living on the street.

DELIA *doesn't respond.*

Look, I'm none the worse for wear and a whole lot smarter than most women will ever be. There's nothing a man can do to surprise me. (*A beat.*) At least I didn't have to wear old-lady suits to work.

DELIA *laughs in spite of herself.*

DELIA. Aren't there any colored gangsters you could fall in love with?

ANGEL. They're married, too, just like the Italians.

SAM *enters and comes upstairs.*

DELIA. That feels wonderful.

ANGEL. See? Those old guys still got their money's worth.

SAM (*standing at the open door*). And that's important to us old guys!

ANGEL. Hey, Doc!

DELIA. Oh! You startled me!

SAM. I'm sorry. I thought we were going to work on your speech.

DELIA. Yes, yes! Of course we are.

She reties her hair back from her face.

SAM (*to* ANGEL). Can you do me?

ANGEL. Sorry. For ladies only. I'll leave you two to your hard work since I can't talk you into coming out to celebrate with us.

SAM. Too bad. What are we not celebrating?

ANGEL. I've got an audition downtown, and Langston's back!

SAM. It's about time. I thought that Negro had put us down for good.

ANGEL. Welcome back party tonight at Bruce's. Guy's across the hall getting his beauty winks right now.

SAM. He'll have to go aways to outshine you in that dress. It looks like it was made for you.

ANGEL. It's Deal's!

SAM (*surprised*). Really?

ANGEL. Turn your back, Doc, so I can return this dress and leave you two in peace.

DELIA (*quickly*). Keep it. You can give it back after your audition.

ANGEL. I'll take good care of it. I promise.

DELIA. I believe you.

ANGEL. And don't pay me any attention, Doc. We promise to have a terrible time without you and, knowing Langston, he probably won't do anything but sit on the fire escape and laugh at everybody.

SAM. Tell him to laugh loud enough for me, will you?

ANGEL *exits to her apartment. She goes into the bedroom to wake* GUY.

SAM. That's a very beautiful dress.

DELIA. It was a gift. I don't know what my aunt was thinking.

A beat. SAM *smiles, but remains at the door.*

If you want to go out, it's all right. I don't want you to feel obligated.

SAM. I'm glad to have a chance to help. May I come in?

DELIA. Of course. I'm sorry. Please… come in.

She starts to close the door, then leaves it partially open. SAM *observes this.*

SAM. If Reverend Powell hadn't told you to ask me, I'd have been forced to volunteer.

DELIA. Why didn't you?

SAM. I thought you might be suspicious of my motives. A middle-aged man with a bad reputation offering to help a beautiful young woman?

DELIA. Do you have a bad reputation?

SAM (*smiling*). In some quarters.

DELIA. Yes... well. Let me take your hat. Sit down.

SAM. Thank you.

DELIA. Why don't I tell you about our planning so far and then you can read what I've been working on?

SAM. I'm all ears.

He suddenly yawns widely.

Please excuse me. I've been working double shifts this week. We're still short-handed.

DELIA. Would you like some coffee?

SAM. Thanks. Maybe that'll wake me up.

As the following scene progresses, DELIA *shows* SAM *some papers, pointing out things to him. She finally hands him a sheaf of pages and, as he reads, she stands up to make coffee. She is trying to give him time to read. We see his head jerk several times. He is trying not to fall asleep. He finally loses the battle, his chin sinks to his chest over the pages in his hand and he sleeps.*

Across the hall, ANGEL *comes out of the bedroom. She is carrying shoes and a shawl. When she comes out, she puts these down and finds the other things she wants among her scattered belongings: several pairs of earrings, other jewelry to try and another pair of shoes. She still has on Delia's dress, but during this scene, she accessorizes it into something so glamorous, it is barely recognizable.* GUY *comes out of the bedroom wearing a beautiful, perfectly cut tuxedo and a formal white shirt. He goes to the mirror and fiddles with his tie.* ANGEL *stands at the mirror too, putting on her make-up.*

ANGEL. Let me do it.

GUY. Don't get lipstick on my collar!

ANGEL. Hold still.

She fixes it expertly.

Voilà!

He slips on his jacket.

GUY. How do I look?

ANGEL. You look positively Parisian!

GUY. Merci, mademoiselle. I'm sorry Deal's not coming, but that dress is perfect for you. I can't believe she let you walk out the door in it.

ANGEL. Sam said it looked like it was made for me.

GUY. That's your special talent. Everybody's clothes look better on you.

ANGEL. I should wear this on Sunday.

GUY. And where are we going on Sunday?

ANGEL. I'm going for a stroll with my mystery man.

GUY. What mystery man?

ANGEL. The guy who walked home with us the other night.

GUY. You saw him again?

ANGEL. He came by Sunday after you all went to Ike Hines's. His name is Leland Cunningham. From Alabama.

GUY. What did he want?

ANGEL. He wanted to make sure I was okay. A real gentleman.

GUY. Which is exactly why you need to leave the boy alone.

ANGEL. He's a grown man. And a good-looking one too.

GUY. All right, 'He's a grown man.' Remember that when he's howling outside the window after you get tired of that down-home charm.

ANGEL. I thought you wanted me to stop hanging around with gangsters.

GUY. I do.

ANGEL. Well, he's definitely not a gangster and we're only going for a walk, if it's okay with you.

GUY. No skin off my nose. I'd have winked at him myself if I thought he was open to persuasion.

ANGEL. Not a chance!

GUY. By the way, who did you tell your country boy I was?

ANGEL. My baby sister.

They exit to the hallway. Delia's door is still partially open.

GUY (*whispering*). Should we let them see how beautiful we are?

ANGEL (*also whispering, but suggestively*). They're working.

She takes his arm and smiles.

We are beautiful, aren't we?

GUY. We are très élégant.

They exit together. Lights back up on DELIA, *pouring two cups of coffee.* SAM's *back is to her. She looks at him expectantly.*

DELIA. Well, what do you think?

SAM *makes no response, and she gets up to walk around to his front. She sees that he is asleep. She is taken aback. At first she is offended, then she is curious, then sympathetic. She sits down across from him and shakes his hand gently. He wakes with a start and blinks guiltily at* DELIA.

SAM. Was I sleeping?

DELIA *nods.*

How long?

DELIA. Long enough.

She takes the pages from where he has dropped them.

Pretty bad, huh?

SAM. No, no! It's my fault. I haven't had much sleep lately.

DELIA. Maybe you should cut back on your nightlife.

SAM. That's the one thing I should not do.

DELIA. And why is that?

SAM. Because it helps me remember that we're not just a bunch of premature labors and gunshot wounds. In a choice between a couple of hours' sleep and a couple of hours of Fats Waller, I'd have to let the good times roll!

DELIA. Don't you ever stop teasing?

SAM. I don't want to work so hard on the body I forget about the soul. (*A beat.*) Besides, I've already cut back on my nightlife. My longtime partners in crime are out right now terrorizing our mutual friends and I'm here with you, working tirelessly to save the race!

DELIA. Maybe not so tirelessly...

SAM. The clinic is a great idea. Your speech is fine and if the good Reverend Powell endorses it, the deacon board probably will too, but...

DELIA. But what?

SAM (*gently*). I deliver babies every day to exhausted women and stone-broke men, but they never ask me about birth control. They ask me about jobs.

DELIA. What does that mean?

SAM. It means we still see our best hope in the faces of our children and it's going to take more than some rich white women playing missionary in Harlem to convince these Negroes otherwise.

DELIA (*angrily*). Why can't we take help wherever we can find it?

SAM. Because it's more complicated than that. The Garveyites are already charging genocide and the clinic isn't even open yet.

DELIA. Genocide?

SAM. And they're not the only ones who feel that way. What does family planning mean to the average colored man? White women teaching colored women how to stop having children.

DELIA. A woman shouldn't have to make a baby every time she makes love!

A beat.

SAM. Is that what you're going to tell those deacons at Abyssinian?

She realizes he has been preparing her for the possibility of these hostile questions from the deacon board. She calms down and answers carefully.

DELIA. No. I'm going to ask them for their help in building strong families with healthy mothers, happy children and loving fathers all over Harlem. Is that better?

SAM (*smiling*). Much better. That's the only approach they can buy. I don't think pleasure is the guiding principle at Abyssinian yet, despite the pastor's best efforts in that direction.

DELIA. Reverend Powell thinks very highly of you. Everyone does.

SAM. Do you?

DELIA. We all do. The work you've done at the hospital... in the community. People are always very impressed that I've met you...

SAM (*embarrassed*). That sounds so respectable, I'm about to make myself sick.

DELIA. You're teasing me again.

SAM. I apologize. It's late. I'd better go.

DELIA. Thank you for your help.

SAM. Now you're teasing me.

DELIA. No. I mean it.

SAM. Did I say something helpful in between resting my eyes?

DELIA. Yes, you did.

SAM. Maybe I was talking in my sleep.

DELIA. Maybe you should try it more often.

SAM. But who'll be there to remember what I say?

DELIA. Goodnight.

SAM. Goodnight.

He exits. DELIA *gathers her papers thoughtfully and gets ready for bed as the lights fade to black.*

Scene Four

Sunday evening. GUY *is sewing on the couch.* ANGEL *enters from the street. She is moving quickly, kicking off her shoes, looking for accessories, changing into Delia's dress again.*

GUY. Where have you been? I thought I was going to have to entertain your beau all by myself.

ANGEL. This is the only day the guys could get together to rehearse for the audition.

GUY. How'd it go?

ANGEL. Great! They sounded so good they make me think I can really sing!

She puts on some very delicate high heels.

I thought you were going to the theatre with Deal.

GUY. We're probably going to miss it, thank God! I do not think my nerves are strong enough for an evening with the literati. Everybody is sure to be abuzz with the news.

ANGEL. What news?

GUY. Bruce and some stallion were holding hands on the street the other night and a group of those young hoodlums knocked the wind out of them for their trouble.

ANGEL. Where were they?

GUY. Right around the corner.

ANGEL. Are they all right?

GUY. Mother and baby both doing fine. Bruce was barefoot, as usual, and they kept trying to stomp on his feet, but he was too quick.

ANGEL. I'm telling you, this Depression is making people mean.

GUY. People been mean. Bruce needs to get himself a straight razor… I thought you two were going for a walk.

ANGEL. We are.

GUY. You're not going very far in those shoes.

ANGEL. Far enough. Where's Deal?

GUY. They changed the deacon's meeting at the last minute. She had to give her speech tonight.

ANGEL. Tonight? Was she ready?

GUY. She was nervous as a cat. Sam went along for moral support.

ANGEL. Good old Sam!

She holds up two different pairs of earrings.

These or these?

GUY. Those.

ANGEL. Do you think so? I thought these might be better with it.

GUY (*exasperated*). Why not wear one of each? What is wrong with you tonight?

ANGEL. The terrible truth is, I don't remember quite what to do when a gentleman comes to call.

GUY. Open the door, extend your hand and drag him in.

She leans to look critically at her face in the mirror. She touches the area around her eyes and at the corners of her mouth and neck.

ANGEL. How old do you think he is?

GUY. Younger than you'd like him to be. Stop worrying. You look beautiful.

ANGEL. The whole time I was going around with Nicky, the whole time I was singing at the Club, I kept thinking something wonderful was going to happen, but it never did. In my mind, I could see myself doing all these things with Nick – riding around in fancy cars, wearing furs, him giving me diamonds. I even saw us getting married. But mostly all we did was go to his place after I'd do the last show. Half the time, his friends would come with us and they'd all sit around drinking and playing cards like I wasn't even there. Then when I'd ask him to take me home, he'd tell me he wanted me to stay around to bring him luck. I remember wishing I could bring myself some luck once in a while. (*A beat.*) This guy feels like luck to me. I don't know why, but he does. That's not so bad, is it?

GUY. Just remember, Sweetie, Alabama isn't just a state. It's a state of mind.

SAM *and* DELIA *enter the building talking excitedly.*

SAM (*laughing*). I thought Deacon Johnson was never going to come around.

DELIA. Until he remembered you delivered all his grandchildren.

GUY. Brace yourself. Here come the rebels.

DELIA (*bursting in, excited*). Sam was wonderful. He convinced everybody…

SAM (*with exaggerated courtliness*)….who hadn't been convinced already by the brilliance of your speech.

DELIA. Tease me as much as you want. We're going to have the best clinic in New York City right up on 126th Street!

SAM. My practice doesn't stand a chance.

GUY. I take it this means you birth-control fanatics will now be free to roam around Harlem at will?

DELIA. Not only that. They're going to list the clinic name, address and services in the church bulletin and I've got an interview with the *Amsterdam News*.

GUY. All that in one night? I am impressed!

SAM. She was amazing. I stayed awake the whole time.

ANGEL. High praise from a man who can sleep anywhere.

SAM. I rose to the occasion.

ANGEL. I'll bet you did!

DELIA. Do you deliver every grandbaby born in Harlem?

SAM. I do my best.

ANGEL. Looks like you owe Doc one, Deal.

DELIA (*flustered*). One what?

GUY. One evening out for dinner with a few of his closest friends.

DELIA. That sounds good to me.

SAM. Me, too, but don't you have tickets to the opening at the Lafayette?

DELIA. I had forgotten all about it!

GUY. Thanks a lot, Doc!

DELIA (*to* SAM). Can you come with us? I'm sure they have tickets left.

GUY. Doc has never stayed awake through a theatrical performance in his life.

SAM. I took a nap this afternoon. I'm good until midnight.

GUY. Well, I stand corrected...

DELIA. Want to come, Angel?

GUY. She can't! She has a gentleman caller arriving momentarily.

DELIA. Really? Who?

ANGEL. His name is Leland Cunningham.

GUY. And he's the prettiest young country thing for miles.

SAM. Is this an official date or just a friendly visit?

ANGEL. We're just going for a walk.

SAM. A Sunday stroll? Angel, this is a new you.

GUY. That's what I told her.

SAM. I can't wait to meet him.

GUY. No time like the present. We've got a minute, don't we, Deal?

DELIA looks at her watch nervously.

Of course we do. He won't be late. No gentleman caller worth the name comes late for a Sunday stroll.

ANGEL. Well, sit down then so you all won't scare him to death the minute he walks in.

GUY. Perfect! We can be casually engaged in pleasant conversation.

A beat. No one can think of a neutral topic.

Okay. I'll start. (*To* ANGEL, *with exaggerated interest.*) Wherever did you get that beautiful dress?

ANGEL. Go to hell!

DELIA. What did you decide to do for your audition?

ANGEL. Thank you! I took your advice. I'm singing blues.

DELIA. I thought you said Italians don't like blues.

ANGEL. They don't have to like blues. They just have to like me. Plus, I'm singing it real fast, almost double-time.

She snaps her fingers and begins to sing while she talks, performing for them. LELAND *enters downstairs and comes up to the door. He checks the number, but before he knocks he listens to her singing.*

And I've got on Deal's beautiful dress, again, and a hat
specifically designed for me by none other than Monsieur
Guy de Paree and I'm dancing just a little and singing the
best I've sung in years and everything is right on time!

She completes the song with a flourish. They applaud as
LELAND *knocks on the door.*

What did I tell you?

ANGEL *goes to the door.* LELAND *immediately removes
his hat. He is wearing a dark suit, a white shirt and a tie.*

Hello, Alabama.

LELAND. Good evening.

ANGEL. Come on in and say hello.

She draws him in.

You met Guy.

GUY. Thanks again for your help the other night.

LELAND. My pleasure.

ANGEL. This is Delia. She lives across the hall. This is her dress.

LELAND. It's beautiful.

DELIA. Thank you.

ANGEL. And this is Sam, but we call him Doc.

LELAND. Are you really a doctor?

SAM. Harlem Hospital. Fifteen years Christmas.

LELAND. It's an honor. I've never met a Negro doctor before.

GUY. Well, stick around. Who knows what else new you might
find!

SAM. Where in Alabama are you from?

LELAND. Tuskegee.

SAM. Home of the world-famous Institute.

LELAND (*pleased*). You're familiar with Dr Washington's work?

SAM. I'm an admirer.

DELIA. I hate to rush everybody, but we're trying to make an eight o'clock curtain.

GUY. The literati wait for no man!

SAM. Good to meet you, Leland.

LELAND. Same here.

GUY. Bye, Sweetie!

SAM, DELIA and GUY exit.

LELAND. I didn't know you were a singer.

ANGEL. You heard me?

LELAND. Through the door.

ANGEL. What did you think I was?

LELAND. Nothing. I mean, I didn't think about you working.

ANGEL. What did you think about me doing?

He doesn't answer, and she laughs at his discomfort.

Do I make you nervous, Alabama?

LELAND. I knew somebody… (*A beat.*) You look a lot like somebody I used to know back home. I keep expecting her voice to come out of your mouth.

ANGEL. Was she your sweetheart?

LELAND. She was my wife. She died eight months ago giving birth to our son. She was always frail, but she said the Lord said be fruitful and multiply and that's what she intended to do. I lost them both.

ANGEL. How long were you married?

LELAND. Two years last May. We grew up together. I knew her all my life.

ANGEL. That's a long time to know somebody and not get tired of them.

LELAND. I couldn't get tired of Anna. It'd be like getting tired of your arms. (*A beat.*) When I passed you and your friend on the street that night, I thought you were a ghost.

ANGEL. Did I look that bad?

LELAND. You looked beautiful. I thought my Anna had come back to me. You've got her eyes, her mouth, her smile...

ANGEL (*interrupting him*). Listen, Alabama, I may look like her, but I'm not her. Don't let's get things confused.

LELAND. I'm not confused. (*A beat.*) I'm real glad to be right here.

ANGEL (*softening*). I didn't mean to snap at you. It's just hard enough to find a gentleman you want to spend some time with and if he's already got another woman's face in his mind, well... (*She shrugs.*) It's still a little hot for a stroll, I think. Would you like to sit here in the window and see if we can catch a breeze?

She gets her fan, and he pulls up two chairs.

LELAND. Are these all right?

ANGEL. Fine.

They sit. As the scene progresses, darkness falls.

I feel like I've been asking all the questions. Now you ask me something.

LELAND. What do you want me to ask?

ANGEL. What do you want to know?

LELAND. Is that really your name?

ANGEL. Yes. My turn again. What are you doing in Harlem?

LELAND. I'm visiting.

ANGEL. Visiting who?

LELAND. Isn't it my turn?

ANGEL. Sorry. Go ahead.

LELAND. Do you ever sing church music?

ANGEL. No. Visiting who?

LELAND. A cousin.

ANGEL. You're not a big talker, huh?

LELAND. I wanted to get out of Tuskegee for a while.
Everybody kept asking me if I was okay about Anna and my
boy. How could I be okay about it? I missed her all the time.
I started feeling like if I turned around real fast, she'd be
standing there, looking at me... laughing the way she used
to... I have a third cousin on my mother's side living up
here. He needed some work done on an old brownstone he
got cheap.

ANGEL. Your cousin bought a brownstone?

LELAND. I sent him a letter and he sent me a train ticket.

ANGEL. One-way or round-trip?

LELAND. I haven't decided yet.

ANGEL. Your turn.

LELAND. Do you have a church home?

ANGEL. A what?

LELAND. A church home. I still haven't found anyplace up
here to...

ANGEL. Try Abyssinian.

LELAND. Is that where you...

ANGEL. I don't go to church.

LELAND. I've already been there.

ANGEL. Didn't you like it?

LELAND. It didn't feel like church to me. The pastor was
talking more about this world then he was the next one.

ANGEL. What should he be talking about?

LELAND (*hesitates, then speaks urgently*). About sin and
salvation. About the presence of hellfire. Reverend Horace,
my pastor back home, says...

ANGEL (*quickly*). Hold on, Alabama.

> LELAND *stops abruptly.*

Church is over for the day, okay?

LELAND. I'm sorry.

ANGEL. Your turn again.

LELAND. I don't know what to ask you.

ANGEL. Ask me what's the worst thing that just happened to me and what's the best one.

LELAND. I can't think about anything bad happening to you.

ANGEL. Twice! Two bad things. Right together. Bam! Bam! Just like that.

LELAND. What were they?

ANGEL. I'm out of a job and I lost all my clothes.

LELAND. Lost your clothes?

ANGEL. Every stitch, except Deal's dress, which doesn't really count, and a few odds and ends I got from Guy.

LELAND. Was there a fire?

ANGEL. Sort of… but the good news is…

> *She waits for him to ask. He's confused and silent. She prompts him.*

'The good news is…'

LELAND. What's the good news?

ANGEL. I've got an audition on Friday and the job is as good as mine!

LELAND. Where do you sing?

ANGEL. In nightclubs. You've been in a juke joint, right?

LELAND. I've seen a couple back home…

ANGEL. Places like that, but with a little more class.

LELAND. Maybe I could come and watch you sometime. Listen to you sing.

ANGEL. It's not going to be church music.

LELAND. Then I won't come on Sunday.

ANGEL. What do you want from me, Alabama?

LELAND. I want to make you laugh.

ANGEL. You talk real pretty for a country boy.

LELAND. The other night, that first night, when you went inside, you dropped this.

He reaches into his pocket and hands her the scarf. She searches his face for a long moment. She raises the scarf to her face, smelling it gently.

ANGEL. It smells like you.

She drapes the scarf around his neck. Straddling his leg, she lowers herself onto his lap slowly as she speaks softly.

Did you take it to bed with you? Did it make you think about me? Was I laughing in your dreams, Alabama?

She kisses him as the lights go to black.

Scene Five

Friday evening. DELIA is standing on a small stool, swathed in a brightly colored piece of silk. The fabric has been draped and wrapped around her by GUY, who is pinning it this way and that distractedly while he talks. DELIA stands with her arms held out stiffly at her sides. There is a transatlantic cable propped underneath the picture of Josephine in the place of honor.

GUY. I knew they'd love my sketches! Now all I have to do is send Josephine three or four finished pieces so they can actually see them on her and... look up, Sweetie!

DELIA. I thought you invited me over here to celebrate.

GUY. I know, I know! But I just had a brilliant idea and I don't want to lose it. Hold still a minute.

DELIA moves her arm and sticks herself.

DELIA. Ow!

GUY *(laughing)*. Your fault!

DELIA. I'll bet you don't stick Angel like that.

GUY. That's because she doesn't squirm, unlike some people who can take the most beautiful fabric in New York City and reduce it to sackcloth over a pinprick or two.

He lifts the fabric off DELIA.

You may step down.

DELIA. Thank you!

GUY *(picking up the cable reverently)*. This is what we've been waiting for, Deal, and it's going to make me crazy until I can tell her everything!

DELIA. Maybe the audition went so well, they asked her to stay and do a show.

GUY. Maybe...

He knows this isn't what happened. He looks at the cable.

Well, hell! Let's pop the cork on this champagne anyway! She can catch up when she gets here.

He pours two glasses, but his mind is still on ANGEL.

We've slowed down now, but me and Miss Angel used to terrorize these streets. When we first got to Harlem, we specialized in gowns for discriminating gentlemen. Don't look so shocked, Deal. You don't think these six-foot queens buy off the rack, do you?

DELIA. I never thought about it.

GUY. Well, I did. The first time I went to the Hamilton Lodge Drag Ball, I knew I was looking at a gold mine. Once they saw Angel in my special creations, I couldn't work fast enough to fill the orders we were getting... Once I made us matching tuxedos. I even painted a little mustache on her.

DELIA. I would have paid to see that.

GUY. I never could make her really look like a man, though. Probably a good thing, too. As it was, she made half the queens who saw her second-guess their stated sexual preference.

DELIA. Did you ever think you and Angel could be... you know...

GUY (*gently*). I like boys, Deal. Remember?

DELIA. Do you think it's because of your grandmother?

GUY. My grandmother wasn't particularly fond of boys, as I recall.

DELIA. I mean being raised by your grandmother. Being so close to her and all...

GUY. Maybe I'm just lucky.

DELIA *yawns widely.*

You keeping Doc's late hours?

DELIA. We're trying to get the clinic open next week and now the landlord says he wants to cancel the lease.

GUY. Why?

DELIA. He got some phone calls, unsigned letters. Now he thinks we're a bunch of free-loving suffragettes out to destroy the Negro race.

GUY (*lightly; he doesn't want to get too serious*). Too late! Mission already accomplished.

DELIA *yawns again.*

DELIA. I'm sorry!

GUY. Don't be sorry. Go get some sleep. We'll continue our celebration later.

DELIA. Goodnight, and congratulations.

GUY. Merci, ma chérie. Bon nuit.

DELIA. Bon nuit.

> DELIA *exits to her apartment, closes the door, yawns again, kicks off her shoes and exits to her bedroom.* GUY *pours himself another glass of champagne, goes to the portrait of Josephine Baker and raises the glass in a toast. He drinks slowly and with great peace and satisfaction.* LELAND *enters, climbs the stairs and knocks at the door. He is carrying a dress box.* GUY *answers.*

GUY. Well, good afternoon. Evening, I guess it is.

LELAND. Good evening. Is Angel here?

GUY. She's not back from the audition yet. You're welcome to come in and wait for her.

LELAND. I can just wait out front.

GUY. Don't be silly. Come on in.

LELAND. Thanks. It is pretty warm out there.

GUY. Want a drink?

LELAND. Is that liquor?

GUY. Champagne.

LELAND. It's still prohibition, isn't it?

GUY. Not in Harlem it isn't, but don't let me corrupt you.

> *He puts on his shirt and tie as they talk.*

> You and Angel doing something special tonight?

LELAND. I'm going to help her celebrate her new singing job.

GUY. Be sure you let her tell you how it went before you pop the cork on that champagne, or whatever it is you do.

LELAND. What do you mean by that?

GUY. I mean it's a rough business. Things don't always go the way you plan them.

LELAND. Thanks. I'll remember that. (*Looking around*.) You a
working man?

GUY. Aren't we all?

LELAND. Not these days. We're two of the lucky ones, I guess.
What do you do?

GUY. Costumes.

LELAND. Like for Halloween?

GUY. No. Nightclubs. Cabarets.

LELAND. People pay you to do that?

GUY. I scrape by. And what do you do?

LELAND. I'm a carpenter.

GUY. Just like Jesus.

LELAND. I didn't mean to offend you. I don't know very much
about show business.

GUY. And I hope you never do.

LELAND. That depends on Angel.

GUY. Then you're home free.

LELAND. Angel told me what happened with her clothes
burning up in the fire and all.

GUY. The fire?

LELAND. At her old place?

GUY. Oh, right. That fire.

LELAND. I know how important clothes are to a woman, so I...

He holds up the box awkwardly.

I bought her something.

GUY. Something to wear?

LELAND. It's a dress, and since she's your cousin and you
know her a lot better than I do, I thought maybe you could
tell me if you think she'll like it.

GUY. Okay. Let's have a look.

GUY *carefully opens the box, folds back the tissue paper and pulls out a long, shapeless navy blue dress with a prim white collar and cuffs. A heart-shaped card falls out.* LELAND *picks the card up quickly before* GUY *can look at it.* GUY *looks at* LELAND*'s hopeful face and speaks gently.*

I think she'll love it.

LELAND. You're not just shining me on, are you?

GUY. I think what she'll like most is that you were thinking about her. Angel likes to know she's on your mind.

He folds the dress carefully and puts it away.

LELAND (*laughing nervously*). Well, no problem there.

GUY. Listen. I just got some good news from Paris and I'm going out to spread joy. You're welcome to stay here and wait for Angel as long as you like. Just do me one favor.

LELAND. If I can.

GUY (*amused*). A healthy suspicion of open-ended questions. I like that in a man.

LELAND (*confused*). Look, I don't think you...

GUY. I don't think anything about anything. As far as I can see, all's right with the world. My dreams are about to come true! Just tell Angel to read that cable, will you? Tell her I tried to wait for her, but I had to answer the call of the wild.

LELAND. I'll tell her.

GUY. No offense.

He extends a hand.

LELAND. None taken.

They shake hands. GUY *exits.* LELAND *walks around looking at everything, touching nothing. He looks out the window. No* ANGEL. *He seats himself to wait.* ANGEL *enters, walking rapidly. She strides into the house angrily.*

LELAND *stands quickly, but she doesn't see him. She grabs the champagne bottle, takes a big gulp, rinses her mouth and spits it into the wastebasket. She tosses the bottle in the same basket and rubs her mouth vigorously with the back of her hand.*

Angel?

She is completely startled.

ANGEL. Are you spying on me?

LELAND. No, we've having dinner, remember?

ANGEL. How did you get in?

LELAND. Guy was here. He told me to tell you... to give you this.

He hands her the cable.

ANGEL. From Josephine?

She grabs it and reads quickly. When she is finished, she speaks sarcastically.

She says she just loves everything, of course. She can't really commit to a job or anything, of course, but if he can just send three or four finished pieces, she's almost certain they might be able to at least think about giving him a try.

She crumples the cable and tosses it down.

LELAND. He said it was a dream come true...

ANGEL. I'm tired of Negro dreams. All they ever do is break your heart.

LELAND (*very gently*). Didn't you sing well?

ANGEL. I never sang at all. Not a note. It wasn't necessary. The job he had open was mine when I hit the front door.

LELAND. I don't understand.

ANGEL. It doesn't matter.

LELAND. Yes, it does. Tell me.

ANGEL. Tony T called the guys and told them the audition was canceled so when I got there, the place was empty. It was just me and him. So he says they must be caught in traffic or something and he offers me a drink while we're waiting and right then, just that quick, I felt it.

LELAND. Felt what?

ANGEL. The truth of it. Me trying to play headliner. Guy trying to play Paris. The whole truth of it. Tony kept saying he could look out for me. Offer me some protection in these hard times. (*A beat.*) He didn't want a singer any more than you do. He wanted to keep a colored woman stashed up in Harlem so he could come by every now and then and rub her head for luck.

LELAND. That son of a…

He reaches for her protectively.

ANGEL. Don't!

LELAND. No Negro woman should have to…

ANGEL. No Negro woman should have to anything, and so what? Do you even understand what I'm talking about? When I was sitting there at Tony's this afternoon, I saw him looking like he could see right through my clothes, and I knew he had talked to Nick about me. I didn't have to imagine what they said. I've heard them talk about women. I know what they say. But I wouldn't let myself think about that. I pushed it right on out of my mind because I know how to take care of myself! I'm not going to be a broke old woman, begging up and down 125th Street, dreaming about fine clothes and French champagne. So, I drank with him and listened to him telling me how long he'd been wanting to get to know me better and I watched him put his hand on my knee like I wouldn't notice and I pretended not to. And I laughed and laughed just to keep up some noise in that room. It was so quiet… Then I stood up to pour another drink and I saw myself in the mirror… and I thought what is that poor, crazy colored woman laughing about? (*A beat.*) When I turned around, there was Tony, waiting for his answer, so I gave it to him…

LELAND. You never have to see him again.

A beat.

ANGEL. We had a good time the other night, Alabama. But the party's over. Go home.

LELAND. I love you.

ANGEL. I don't love you.

LELAND. But you will. You had a run of bad luck, but it's over now. I'm going to take care of you.

ANGEL. Why? So you can call me by some other woman's name?

A beat.

LELAND. I know you're not my Anna. I know that! But I still have all the love she gave me. And if I can't shape it new to protect and cherish and keep you, if I can't save you any more then I could save her, then that love isn't worth a damn thing.

ANGEL. All I can do for you is drive you crazy.

LELAND. You can't drive me anyplace I don't want to go.

ANGEL (*suddenly overwhelmed*). I'm tired.

LELAND (*picking up his hat*). Should I come tomorrow?

ANGEL. Yes.

LELAND. Goodnight, then.

A beat.

ANGEL. Goodnight.

As he starts out the door, she calls out to him.

Leland?

He turns to her. She tries to smile.

You gonna be my lucky charm?

LELAND. I'm gonna be your man.

He turns and exits downstairs. She closes the door and leans against it wearily. She sees the dress box, opens it, picks up the card and reads it, folds back the tissue paper and looks at the dress. She sees how horrible it looks, sighs in resignation, withdraws it from the box slowly and holds it up against her body as the lights go to black.

ACT TWO

Scene One

*Two weeks later. It is early Sunday afternoon. Things are
arranged for a 'high tea' to celebrate Guy's readiness to mail
his costumes to Paris. There are flowers, china plates and cups
arranged on a silver tray. Guy's package of costumes, wrapped
for mailing, is sitting under the photo of Josephine as if waiting
for a blessing. ANGEL is putting out spoons and napkins. She
is wearing the dress Leland gave her, but she has improved
upon it slightly with a belt or other visible adjustments. GUY
enters downstairs. He is wearing tuxedo pants, a formal shirt
with an ascot and a silk smoking jacket. He is disheveled. He is
carrying a small bag from the grocery store. He bursts into the
apartment angrily. He puts down the bag and goes to the mirror
to check himself for damages.*

ANGEL. What happened to you?

GUY. Young hoodlums down the street trying to prove their
manhood.

ANGEL. Are you all right? You're bleeding!

GUY. Where?

He checks himself, then grins.

No, I'm not. But somebody is! Damn! This shirt is brand-new!

*He makes sure the jacket covers the small stain, reties his
ascot and smoking jacket sash as they talk.*

ANGEL (*relieved*). You scared me to death!

GUY. Relax, Sweetie! If you ever see me in a fight with a bear,
you help the bear.

ANGEL. I can't believe these Negroes are out robbing people
on Sunday morning.

GUY. They weren't robbing me. They didn't like the way I was dressed. I was a little too continental for their uncouth asses.

ANGEL. Did you recognize any of them?

GUY. What difference does it make? They are a temporary inconvenience. In Paris, a well-turned gentleman does not have to be subjected to the barbarism of street thugs!

He finishes his neatening up.

Good as new! And, I didn't drop the sugar!

He takes it out of the bag and fills the china sugar bowl.

ANGEL. I wish you'd be more careful.

GUY. Walking up to the corner in broad daylight?

ANGEL. Leland knows some of these guys and he said...

GUY. What guys?

ANGEL. Like the ones who... stopped you at the store.

GUY. They didn't stop me. They offered to kick my ass.

ANGEL. You know they'll spot you dressed like that!

GUY. Spot me? I'm not hiding! Look, I'm leaving this place as fast as I can, but until I do? I plan to walk where I please, wearing what I please, whenever I please. What's Leland doing hanging around with those hoodlums anyway?

ANGEL. He just met some of them at a prayer meeting or something...

GUY. Nothing like a God-fearing man.

ANGEL. I don't know what I'd do if something happened to you.

GUY. Likewise, I'm sure.

A beat.

ANGEL. I talked to Bobby last week.

GUY. Lucky you.

ANGEL. When were you going to tell me they fired you?

GUY. As the ship pulled away from the dock and not a minute before.

ANGEL. Don't you think I have a right to know?

GUY. Why? So you can worry yourself to death and drive me crazy?

ANGEL. I'm serious!

GUY. I'm serious too! I've been working like a young slave to get this stuff ready for Josephine. I'm sewing for whatever clubs are left in Harlem and I got two weddings coming up if all else fails. We'll make it, Angel. I promise.

ANGEL. You're a hell of a provider, Big Daddy.

GUY. You wouldn't dismiss it all so fast if I was a straight man offering to take you to Paris.

ANGEL. But you're not that, are you?

SAM *and* DELIA *arrive.*

GUY. Bonjour! Bonjour! Comment ça va? Comment ça va?

He kisses DELIA *on both cheeks.*

DELIA. Everything looks beautiful.

SAM. I've never been invited to high tea before. I didn't know Negroes were allowed to partake.

GUY. I won't tell if you don't tell.

SAM. So when is the great international launch actually taking place?

GUY. I'm going to put this package containing five – count 'em! – five, brand-new, breathtaking, Guy de Paree originals on a freighter tomorrow morning at ten o'clock, then hold my breath for three weeks!

DELIA. Tell him about Langston's friend.

GUY. Langston knows a Negro in Paris who has a lover at the French Embassy. He'll come to pick it up so it won't get held up in customs.

DELIA. Langston had to promise him that he could personally deliver the package to Josephine.

SAM. He'll probably arrive in top hat and tails.

GUY. All of Josephine's admirers arrive in top hat and tails!

SAM. Why so quiet, Angel Eyes? Cat got your tongue?

ANGEL. I hate that expression.

GUY. Angel and I have been fighting about my effectiveness as a provider.

SAM. A provider of what?

ANGEL. Let's talk about something else.

DELIA. Is Leland coming?

ANGEL. Any minute now.

SAM. Should I be asking about this Negro's intentions?

GUY. Maybe you should ask him if he's a good provider.

SAM. He seems to be an honest, hard-working man. You can't hardly ask for more than that, can you?

LELAND *enters downstairs.*

DELIA. Do you love him?

GUY. Out of the mouths of babes!

LELAND *knocks on the door.*

ANGEL. Sh-h-h-h!

She opens the door for LELAND.

LELAND. Good afternoon.

ANGEL. Good afternoon yourself. Come in and say hello to everybody.

LELAND. Hello, everybody.

SAM. Good to see you again.

LELAND. Thank you. Miss Patterson...

DELIA. Call me Delia.

GUY. We were just talking about you.

LELAND. I hope some good things were said on my behalf.

ANGEL. The best. Sit down.

There is an awkward silence.

LELAND. I seem to have interrupted something.

SAM (*quickly*). We were just congratulating Delia. Margaret Sanger addressed the congregation at Abyssinian this morning.

GUY. I completely forgot this was the day! I have been working too hard. Sorry, sorry, sorry! Tell me everything.

DELIA. I don't think Margaret had ever been around that many colored people at one time, but she was wonderful!

SAM. She even had a couple of converts in the amen corner.

LELAND. I'm sorry to have to ask, but who is she?

DELIA. She's an advocate for family planning. She has two clinics in New York already and now we're going to open one right here in Harlem.

GUY. They'll probably put Doc out of business in a couple of years. Tea, or shall we just put some gin in these cups and call it square?

SAM. Is that why they call it high tea?

LELAND. You're talking about birth control, aren't you?

DELIA. Aren't you in favor of it?

GUY. I vote for the gin. How about you, Doc?

LELAND. The cure for mothers who don't want babies is fathers who do.

ANGEL. What else happened at Abyssinian? Was Isabel there?

GUY. Did she sit in the third pew on the right and gaze at Adam Junior like he just hung the moon?

SAM. From the expression on his face when she walked down the center aisle, I don't think Reverend Powell Senior has resigned himself to having a showgirl in the family.

GUY. Isabel can always be counted on for high drama.

ANGEL. She told me the most romantic story I've ever heard.

DELIA. I didn't know you knew Isabel Washington.

ANGEL. We were in the Cotton Club chorus together. Then she got that part in a Broadway show where Adam saw her and they fell in love.

GUY. L'amour, l'amour!

ANGEL. He was still in school up at Colgate and his father was determined to keep them apart.

LELAND. Every woman is not cut out to be a pastor's wife.

There is an awkward silence.

SAM. I'll say amen to that!

ANGEL. They had a big fight about something and all the way up there on the train, she was planning to break off their relationship for good. By the time the train pulled into the station, it was dark outside and snow was starting to fall.

GUY. High drama!

DELIA. Go on, Angel!

ANGEL. Even worse, she didn't see Adam at all. She was fit to be tied. She grabbed her suitcase, determined to catch the next train back to Harlem, but when she stepped onto the platform, there he was at the end of it with snow in his hair and his arms full of long-stemmed red roses.

GUY. You've got to be born with a talent for finding roses in the middle of December!

ANGEL. He walked the length of the platform...

GUY. And knowing Isabel, she waited right there for him to walk it, too!

ANGEL. Then he dropped the roses at her feet, swept her up in his arms and kissed her right there for all the world to see. (*A beat.*) And they've been together ever since.

DELIA. Snow roses!

GUY. Snow job is more like it. (*Melodramatically, as if reading from a bad novel.*) And in the sudden darkness, he felt that he was lost inside her.

DELIA. What's the most romantic thing you ever saw?

GUY. I thought you'd never ask! It was just the other night so it's fresh in my mind. Angel was there.

ANGEL. Where?

GUY. Langston's party at Bruce's place.

ANGEL (*nervously*). That's too new to qualify as a memory.

GUY. The question was what is the most romantic thing you ever saw. Is there a statute of limitations?

SAM. Not that I know of. Fire when ready.

GUY. There were a million people there. Young and not so young. Rich and poor. Well, not that poor. You know Bruce is a snob. But everyone was acting very sophisticated and unimpressed with the stars who were floating around. The beautiful young men in their own tuxedos were arranged at strategic points throughout the room, as usual, but their attention was focused on a tall, slender young man with a poetic mouth and the body of a sepia Adonis. They couldn't hardly welcome Langston home for eyeballing this handsome stranger, when in walks…

LELAND. Excuse me. The men were looking at another man?

ANGEL. Maybe you should save this story for another time. You tell one, Deal.

LELAND. I just don't think I understood you right. Did you say these men at your party were making…

GUY. It wasn't my party. I was a guest. Just like Angel.

LELAND (*to* ANGEL). Did you see those men looking at that other man?

ANGEL. It was just a party, Leland. Nothing happened.

LELAND. What did you mean when you said eyeballing?

SAM. Maybe I can...

GUY. Eyeballing. Admiring. Sizing up. Flirting.

LELAND. Men flirting with men?

GUY. They were homosexuals, for God's sake. What's wrong with you?

LELAND. Don't put God's name in the stuff you're talking about! I don't know how sophisticated New York people feel about it, but in Alabama, there's still such a thing as abomination!

GUY (*standing*). Get out.

ANGEL. Guy! Don't!

GUY. Then I think you better.

ANGEL (*looking at* LELAND *helplessly*). Will you wait for me downstairs for just a minute, honey?

LELAND *hesitates*.

I'll be right down. I promise. Please?

LELAND (*stiffly*). Good afternoon, Miss Patterson. Dr Thomas.

LELAND *exits*.

SAM. I'll talk to him.

SAM *exits*. DELIA *goes quietly with him and, with a look to the others that acknowledges the awkward moment, goes to her apartment.* SAM *goes downstairs to where* LELAND *stands stiffly by the stoop. Upstairs,* GUY *and* ANGEL *face each other angrily.*

GUY. He's exactly the kind of small-minded, ignorant, judgmental bastard I left Savannah to get away from!

ANGEL. He didn't deserve that!

GUY. Who gave him the right to vote on my love stories?

ANGEL. Who gave you the right to vote on mine?

SAM and LELAND are talking on the stoop.

SAM (*to* LELAND). I'll tell you, Brother Leland, we're an opinionated group of loud talkers, but we truly do love Angel.

LELAND. I would die for Angel.

SAM. Live for her, man. It's a much better bargain.

LELAND. I just don't believe in those things they were talking about. (*A beat.*) Do they kill babies at that clinic, too?

SAM. No.

LELAND. There was a white doctor at home used to do that when girls got in trouble. Their mamas would bring them to the back door after hours. I thought a doctor was supposed to save lives.

SAM. It's not always that clear a question.

LELAND. You don't do those operations, do you?

A beat.

SAM. It's against the law.

LELAND. That doesn't seem to matter up here! Isn't it against the law for one man to eyeball another man?

SAM. Didn't you know Guy was homosexual?

LELAND. She said he was her second cousin from home. She didn't say anything about him being that way and I never thought to ask her. Did you know he was that way?

SAM. Of course. We've been friends for ten years.

LELAND. You're not...?

SAM. No, but you're not going to meet a better man than Guy. He's saved Angel's life more than once and probably mine, too.

LELAND. You call him a man, the same as you or me?

SAM. He is a man.

LELAND. Well, he may be what you call a man, but he ain't the same as me and the sooner I get Angel out of there, the better it will be for all of us. Would you please tell her I'll be back later?

SAM. All right.

LELAND. I'm surprised you can accept something like that.

SAM. I'm just a doctor. I'm not God.

LELAND *exits. They are still arguing upstairs.*

ANGEL. Sometimes I think you're jealous.

GUY. I'm always jealous, but I just don't get what you see in this guy.

ANGEL. A rent check that won't bounce.

GUY. Is that it?

ANGEL. Isn't that enough?

GUY. Listen, Sweetie, everything's about to change. As soon as Josephine's producer sees these costumes, they're going to send me a ticket as fast as they can get to the American Express office. Come with me, Angel! Paris is another world away from here. Everywhere you've been looking lately there's nothing but a bunch of sad-eyed souls wondering who pulled the rug out. But Paris won't be like this. I promise. We'll sleep on satin and dress in silk and drink so much fine French champagne we'll get tired of it.

ANGEL. I can't go to Paris with you. You love me, but you don't want to take me home.

GUY. I always take you home.

ANGEL *(only half teasing)*. But you can't get lost inside me.

GUY *(surprised)*. Do you want me to?

ANGEL. I've thought about it.

GUY *is a little uncomfortable with the turn the conversation has taken.*

GUY. I've thought about it, too, but you're just not my type.

ANGEL. Leland wants to take care of me. I'm going to let him try.

GUY. You don't love him.

ANGEL. He'll never know the difference.

GUY. Yes, he will.

ANGEL. And then what?

GUY. He'll never be able to forgive you for the lie.

ANGEL. Just like you.

GUY. No. I forgive you everything. That's what we've always traded.

ANGEL. And why is that?

GUY. Because you let me see how beautiful I was.

SAM *enters alone.*

ANGEL. Where's Leland?

SAM. He said he'll be back later.

ANGEL. Maybe I can catch him.

She exits quickly.

GUY. The story of my life, Doc. Always the bridesmaid, never the bride. You want to finish this high tea with me?

SAM. I thought I might look in on your neighbor.

GUY. L'amour, l'amour! Well, I'm too pretty to spend Sunday afternoon all alone. I think I'll go over to the Kit Kat Klub and see what trouble I can get into.

SAM. You know I had your back earlier.

GUY. I'd-a sliced that country fool six ways 'til Sunday.

SAM. Maybe we'll catch up with you later.

GUY. I wouldn't count on it.

GUY *exits behind* SAM, *who taps on Delia's door. She answers immediately.*

SAM. The coast is clear. May I come in?

DELIA. Of course.

She doesn't close the door completely.

Did you talk to Leland?

SAM. I did. He thinks we're a bunch of amoral Philistines.

DELIA. I don't know anybody like him.

SAM. Most of the people I see think like that.

DELIA. About birth control?

SAM. About life.

DELIA. What do you say to them?

SAM. I ask the mother if she is watching her diet. I tell the father to bring her fruit instead of candy.

DELIA. I mean about what they think.

SAM. Nothing.

DELIA. So now what?

SAM. She's going to break his heart.

DELIA. Leland or Guy?

SAM. Both.

DELIA. I don't want to be in love like that.

SAM. Do you want to be in love?

DELIA. Yes. Don't you?

SAM. How old are you?

DELIA. Angel says once you're grown, what difference does it make?

SAM. And are you grown?

DELIA. There's no way to answer a question like that.

SAM. There's no way to answer the one you asked me either.

DELIA. That one should be easy.

SAM. I'm forty years old. I work too hard and I drink too much.

DELIA. But would you like to be in love?

SAM. I've been waiting all my life to be in love.

DELIA. Me, too.

She kisses SAM *gently.*

SAM. May I close the door?

DELIA. Yes.

SAM. Should I lock it?

DELIA. Yes.

SAM. Good.

DELIA. I didn't think I'd be so nervous. I talk about this all the time. Not specifically about you, of course, just in general.

SAM. Don't worry about a thing. I'm a doctor.

DELIA. I know everything about birth control.

SAM. Good.

DELIA. But, I mean, it's all theoretical. I've never...

SAM. Do you want to get married first?

DELIA. I thought we were talking about falling in love.

SAM. We are.

DELIA. I promised myself I'd never marry a doctor.

SAM. I'll stop practicing. I'll wear two-tone shoes and play the baritone sax.

A beat.

DELIA. Will you do everything real slow?

SAM. As molasses...

He puts his arm around her, and they exit to the bedroom.
ANGEL *enters and sits on the stoop.* LELAND *enters
almost immediately and stands watching* ANGEL, *who looks
up suddenly to see him standing there.*

ANGEL. I thought maybe you weren't coming back.

LELAND. I wasn't sure you wanted me to.

ANGEL (*teasing gently*). You think I'd be sitting out here in my
new dress if I didn't?

LELAND. No, I guess you wouldn't. (*A beat.*) What did you do
to it?

ANGEL. I just fixed it up a little. Don't you like it?

LELAND. I liked it the way it was before.

ANGEL. Come here.

She stands, embraces him and then steps back, surprised.

What's that?

LELAND (*removing a pistol from his waistband*). I'm sorry.
I went by to check on my cousin's place and I always...

He sticks the gun in the back of his belt quickly.

You never know who's gonna walk up on you in Harlem.
A man has to be prepared, even on Sunday!

ANGEL. I hate guns.

A beat.

LELAND. Listen, Angel, I'm not like you and your friends.
I believe there's a right and a wrong of it.

ANGEL. Guy's family.

LELAND. That doesn't make it right!

ANGEL. I think you're just scared.

LELAND. Scared of what? We had his kind back home, but we
didn't hang around with them.

ANGEL. And what kind is that?

LELAND. I told you I was a God-fearing, Christian man the first time you ever laid eyes on me.

ANGEL. I thought you said you weren't afraid of anything.

LELAND. Reverend Horace, my pastor back home, he said sometimes when we think we hear the voice of God, it isn't that at all. It's something else, something we want to put up in God's place, like money or lust or gambling. He said sometimes the voice of that other thing can sound so sweet, we swear it's the heavenly choir. But it's not.

A beat.

ANGEL. You know what I'm afraid of? Nothing so grand as losing my soul, of course. All I'm afraid of is trying to lean on one more weak Negro who can't finish what he started!

LELAND hesitates, starts to speak, changes his mind. He exits. ANGEL watches him go as the lights go to black.

Scene Two

Two weeks later. SAM is sitting patiently on the stoop outside the apartment. ANGEL enters. She is wearing the same dress she had on at the start of the play, but it, and she, look a bit worse for wear. She is pleased to see SAM.

ANGEL. Hey, Doc.

SAM. You're a sight for sore eyes. Where are you going all dressed up?

ANGEL sits beside him.

ANGEL. I've been where I'm going, and just between me and you? It doesn't pay as good as it used to.

SAM. Things are tough all over.

She takes off her high heels and rubs her feet.

ANGEL. How did we ever get this old?

SAM. One day at a time. Brother Leland still missing in action?

ANGEL. I must have been crazy to let that Alabama Negro walk out of here.

SAM. Your test came back.

A beat.

ANGEL. How far gone am I?

SAM. Almost eight weeks.

ANGEL. Well, it never rains but it pours, right?

SAM. I'm sorry this isn't what you want.

ANGEL. Yeah. Me, too. (*A beat.*) What are you doing out here, anyway?

SAM. Deal's still down at the clinic. That woman works so hard, I barely see enough of her to be a bad influence.

ANGEL. Well, come on upstairs. Maybe I can scare us up something to drink.

SAM. Not me. I've got to go back to the hospital, but...

ANGEL sees an official notice tacked to the door. She takes it down and reads it with some agitation.

SAM. What is it?

ANGEL. It's an eviction notice. We're going to be set out on the street!

SAM. Let me see it.

He reads the notice. It confirms what ANGEL *has said.*

ANGEL. Guy told me he paid it two weeks ago!

SAM. It might be a mistake. Why don't you wait and see what Guy says?

ANGEL (*angrily*). What does he ever say? Comment ça va? Comment ça va?

SAM. I can probably come up with fifty or sixty bucks. (*Apologetically.*) My patients clean me out the first of every month, but...

ANGEL. I'll figure something out.

She turns away from him.

SAM. Okay, Angel Eyes. Call me if you need me.

SAM *exits.* ANGEL *goes to her purse, opens it, dumps out the contents and separates out the money. There are only a few bills and some coins. She checks to make sure she didn't miss anything. She didn't. She stuffs the money back into her purse. She is not pleased. She picks up the notice again and looks at it as if the intensity of her gaze could change the words.* GUY *enters carrying an armful of flowers.*

GUY. Bonjour, chérie! Comment ça va? Look at these! I couldn't resist them.

ANGEL. Have you seen this?

GUY *reads the notice, lays the flowers near* ANGEL.

GUY. Sorry, Sweetie. I'll take care of it.

ANGEL. With what? How much have you got?

GUY. Almost enough.

ANGEL. Almost enough?

GUY. I never said my name was Rockefeller. How much have you got?

ANGEL. Fourteen dollars and seventy-two cents.

GUY. Every little bit helps. Don't worry. Big Daddy is on the case. I've been feeling Josephine in the air all day!

ANGEL. Stop it! Just stop it! Don't you understand? They're going to put us out on the street in seven days! One week!

GUY. Then I better hustle on down to the cable office and see if there's anything there for me.

ANGEL. Whatever presence you're feeling hasn't got anything to do with Josephine. We're not in Paris. We're in Harlem. We're not strolling the boulevard. We're about to be evicted!

A beat.

GUY. Do you want to walk down with me? Maybe we can scare up some dinner.

ANGEL. I think it's time for me to look out for myself. (*Sarcastically.*) Big Daddy.

GUY. You always do, Angel. One way or another.

He exits.

ANGEL *begins to cry in anger and frustration.* LELAND *enters, comes upstairs and knocks gently. She opens the door and looks at him. He is the last person she wants to see.*

ANGEL. What do you want?

She turns away from him and he follows her.

LELAND. Angel, please, listen to me...

ANGEL. I'm listening.

A beat.

LELAND. The night I found you, I went to bed early, like I always do, but I couldn't sleep. I was just laying there, wide awake. So I got up and went out for a walk. I was missing that Alabama sky where the stars are so thick it's bright as day. So, I looked up between the buildings and I thought I was dreaming. Didn't even look like Harlem. Stars everywhere, twinkling at me like a promise. And then I saw you. And that was all I saw. Just you. (*A beat.*) Marry me, Angel. I'll never leave you again.

ANGEL. Swear it.

LELAND. I swear it.

ANGEL. I was hoping you would come.

LELAND. You were?

ANGEL. Yes. I want your son to grow up with his father.

LELAND. What did you say?

ANGEL. We're going to have a child.

LELAND. Are you sure?

ANGEL. I'm sure.

LELAND (*suddenly agitated*). What time is it?

ANGEL. About four, I think...

LELAND. We can get the license today!

ANGEL. Now?

LELAND. Right now! I think this is our lucky day. Don't you?

ANGEL. Maybe you can convince me.

He quickly embraces her as the lights go to black.

Scene Three

The next day. SAM and DELIA are in her apartment. DELIA is quite agitated.

SAM. It's not going to do any good to get yourself all worked up again.

DELIA. Somebody could have been killed!

SAM. But nobody was.

DELIA. You know what some of them are telling Margaret, don't you? They're telling her to forget about a clinic in Harlem. It's too dangerous.

SAM. Not if we move it someplace safer.

DELIA. Everybody knows that fire was set to run us out. Who's going to rent to us now?

SAM. I am.

DELIA. What are you talking about?

SAM. The ground floor of my parents' brownstone was my first office when I got out of medical school. It's not very big, but it's completely independent of the house with an entrance on the street, three examining rooms and some basic equipment.

DELIA. How long would it take to get it ready for patients?

SAM. Probably the end of the week with what's already there and what you can salvage from your place.

DELIA. That would show them something, wouldn't it?

SAM (*embracing her protectively*). You can't let them think they scared you!

DELIA (*laughing with relief*). They did scare me!

GUY *enters from outside. He is resplendent in new hat, suit, shoes and spats. He is carrying a bottle of champagne and an overseas cable. He takes the steps two at a time and bursts upon DELIA and SAM.*

GUY. Listen to this! (*Reading from the cable.*) 'To Mr Guy Jacobs…'

DELIA. You heard from Josephine?

GUY. Just sit down and listen!

DELIA. All right, all right!

GUY. 'To Mr Guy Jacobs…'

SAM. You already read that part!

GUY (*with great dignity*). I'm starting from the beginning so you two can get the full effect, unless you haven't got the time to hear the words that are going to change my life forever.

DELIA. We'll be quiet. I promise!

GUY. 'To Mr Guy Jacobs, Harlem, New York, from Mademoiselle Josephine Baker, the Folies Bergère, Paris, France. Ma chérie…' Ma chérie… music to my ears!

DELIA. Read it!

GUY. 'Ma chérie, your costumes fabulous! All here green with envy. Must use all five in next show.' Can you believe it? All five!

SAM. Go on, man! You're killing me!

GUY. 'Looking forward to seeing you in Paris as soon as you can make the crossing! Au revoir, ma chérie! Je t'aime! Je t'aime! Je t'aime!' She wrote that three times and she sent a first-class ticket and enough cash to get whatever I need for the trip, including this beautiful ensemble. Get the glasses!

DELIA. I don't have any.

GUY. You're hopeless! Follow me!

They go across the hall. GUY *gets glasses.*

She said they loved everything. Every single piece fit perfectly.

SAM. Of course they did. You're a genius.

GUY. I'm a realist. I added two inches to the measurements she sent me! Women always lie about their ages and their hips!

DELIA. And what do men lie about?

GUY. Men lie about everything else. (*Toasting the photograph.*) To Josephine, the magnificent! Merci, merci, merci! It is my intention to run the streets of Harlem tonight until everyone who ever crossed me has heard the news and turned pea green with envy. I will expect you two to accompany me if I'm going to have any chance of returning home alive.

SAM. I would consider it an honor as well as my sacred duty as your personal physician!

DELIA. I wouldn't miss it.

SAM. Let the good times roll!

DELIA. I need to change.

GUY. Thank God. That suit has a life of its own, but it's not a nightlife.

DELIA. I'll just be a minute.

SAM. Don't rush. I have to stop by the hospital, anyway.

GUY. Why don't you meet us at Ike Hines's? We'll start the evening with some celebratory chop suey and see where the spirit leads us!

SAM. If I'm not back in ten minutes, I'll meet you there by eight-thirty.

DELIA. Be careful.

SAM. Careful as I can.

He kisses her and exits.

GUY. L'amour, l'amour!

DELIA. Have you told Angel?

GUY. I haven't seen her.

DELIA. She won't believe it.

GUY. She'll believe it when I hand her first-class passage to Paris. Then she can stop looking out the window for that long-gone Alabama fool like he's her ticket to Paradise.

DELIA. This suit isn't that bad, is it?

GUY. Worse than that, but what the hell? Maybe I'll send you back a dress from Paris.

DELIA. Would you?

GUY. I'll send a dozen dresses, all with shoes to match and tiny little hats with veils.

DELIA. I always wanted to see Paris.

GUY. In the springtime?

DELIA. Anytime. I won't be but a minute.

GUY. Good! I'm ready to move out amongst 'em!

DELIA *exits to her apartment bedroom to change.* GUY *pours himself another glass of champagne.* ANGEL *enters wearing* LELAND's *dress without adornment and very little make-up.*

Comment ça va, chérie?

He kisses her on both cheeks.

That dress is more dreadful every time I see it, but all is forgiven!

ANGEL. Where did you spend last night? Shoplifting at Saks Fifth Avenue?

GUY. I didn't get there 'til this morning and I paid cold, hard cash.

ANGEL. Well, it must have been a big night.

GUY. Bigger than that. Are you ready?

ANGEL. I want to tell you something...

GUY. My news first!

ANGEL. All right, go ahead.

GUY. I heard from Josephine. They are going to use every single piece I sent them, and she sent so much real live spending money that I was able to pay off everybody we owe and still purchase you first-class passage to Gay Paree!

He hands her a folder with the necessary papers and tickets.

We sail a week from Friday! Now aren't you glad I made you get your passport? Otherwise we'd have to wait a month and you know how mean Josephine gets when you keep her waiting! Don't look so surprised. Say something!

ANGEL. You're really going.

GUY. We're going.

ANGEL *does not respond.*

Aren't we?

ANGEL. Bad timing, Big Daddy. I'm pregnant.

A beat.

GUY. Accident or insurance?

ANGEL. Yes.

GUY. Does Leland know?

ANGEL. He asked me to marry him. And I told him I would.

GUY. Well, I guess we missed the moment big time, didn't we?

A beat.

ANGEL. No, we didn't. I don't even love him! You said so yourself!

GUY. What about the baby? What about Leland?

ANGEL. I can get rid of it! I'm not that far along! I'll tell him I had a miscarriage.

GUY. So you're going to tell him you miscarried his baby and oh, by the way, the wedding is off because you're sailing for France next Friday?

ANGEL. I thought you were the one who could forgive me everything.

He takes the folder and lays it on the table beside her.

GUY. Sometimes you wear me out, Miss Angel. Sometimes you just wear me out.

He closes the door behind him as DELIA *steps out into the hallway. He smiles at her.*

Ready?

DELIA. How do I look?

GUY. We'll work on it.

They exit out the back door of the building as SAM *enters downstairs.* ANGEL *picks up the ticket and holds it in her hand. She savors the possibilities that it represents. It is clear that she has already settled the questions involved and is headed for Paris.* SAM *sticks his head in the door.*

SAM. Did I miss the celebrants?

ANGEL. They just left.

SAM. I was hoping I could catch them. You've heard the big news?

ANGEL *nods*.

SAM. So how is it, Angel Eyes?

ANGEL. It's been better. (*A beat*.) Leland came by last night.

SAM. Is that good or bad?

ANGEL. He asked me to marry him.

SAM. So you two patched things up after all?

ANGEL. I don't want to have this baby, Sam.

A beat.

SAM. What about Leland?

ANGEL. What about him? (*A beat*.) I don't know. I just know
I'm going to Paris. Guy booked passage for me and we sail
next Friday.

SAM. Did you tell him about the baby?

ANGEL. Of course I told him. He was surprised at first, maybe
a little mad at me. He sounded like you. 'What about
Leland? What about Leland?' What about me?

SAM. This will kill him, Angel.

ANGEL. No, it won't! He'll live through it just fine. And so
will I. (*A beat*.) This is my chance to live free, Doc, and I'm
taking it.

SAM. Freedom's such an abstract thing. That baby's flesh and
blood.

A beat.

ANGEL. It was flesh and blood the last time, too, but it didn't
seem to bother you. What's the difference? How come a little
half-Italian baby didn't tug at your heartstrings like this one
does?

SAM. It wasn't the same thing.

ANGEL. Yes, it was. I was carrying a baby I didn't want from a
man I didn't love and I wanted to get rid of it without
bleeding to death on somebody's kitchen table.

SAM. You told me you'd go crazy if you had to have Nick's child.

ANGEL. Is that what you want? Then will you save me?

SAM. You're asking me to do something I don't think I'm prepared to do.

A beat.

ANGEL. So is that how it works? You can help as long as the poor, ignorant woman is at her wit's end and could never survive the birth. As long as all she's going to do after you save her is go home and feel guilty enough or scared enough to keep the next one so you can deliver it and bring us all a bottle of champagne to toast the newest citizens of Harlem... and let the good times roll? (*A beat.*) Don't worry about it. I'm sure Tony T can find me a number if I tell him that the baby's his.

SAM. It doesn't have to be this hard.

ANGEL. It already is, Doc. Just not for you.

A beat.

SAM. I'll be in my office tomorrow morning first thing.

ANGEL. Why? Because I made you feel guilty?

SAM. Because you're right. Everybody's got to kill their own snakes.

ANGEL. Thanks, Doc. I'll never ask you again. I promise!

SAM *sits wearily.*

What have we got to drink around here?

She rummages through the cabinets as SAM *watches her. The lights fade to black.*

Scene Four

The following day. It is mid-morning. GUY *is hanging up some costumes prior to delivering them.* ANGEL *enters. She is walking slowly. She comes upstairs and enters the apartment.*

GUY. You're out early. I didn't even hear you get up.

ANGEL. I took care of it.

GUY. What are you talking about?

ANGEL. I saw Sam.

GUY. This morning?

ANGEL. Just now. (*A beat.*) There is no more baby.

GUY. My God, Angel! Did he bring you home?

ANGEL. I caught a cab. He's coming by later.

GUY. Do you want to lie down? Can I get you anything?

ANGEL. I'm all right.

GUY. My God, Angel!

ANGEL. Stop saying that!

She sits down and closes her eyes wearily.

GUY. I'm taking the last of these costumes over to the club, but I'll be right back. Will you be okay?

ANGEL. You're not sorry, are you?

GUY. Are you?

ANGEL. I'm sorry in about twenty different ways and I don't give a damn about any of them.

GUY. I won't be long.

He exits. ANGEL *remains motionless, eyes closed.* LELAND *enters, carrying a small rocking chair. He struggles up the stairs with it and knocks on Angel's door. She opens the door, and is startled to see the chair in front of her.*

ANGEL. Oh! I thought it was Sam.

LELAND. May I come in?

ANGEL. Of course.

LELAND (*putting the chair down gently*). It's a rocking chair.

He rocks it.

I made it for you. I started on it that first night I saw you...

ANGEL *stops the chair from rocking.*

ANGEL. My grandmother said death rocks an empty chair!

LELAND. Then sit in it. I want you to rock all of our children in this chair.

ANGEL turns away quickly, but LELAND *embraces her.*

I just came from my cousin's place. I had those guys hoppin' up there today! We're going to be able to move in a lot sooner then I thought. Maybe next month. Right after the wedding. Would you like that?

ANGEL. Yes, I...

LELAND. And, I have something else for you.

He reaches into his pocket and brings out a small box.

Open it.

She opens it. Inside is a small diamond ring.

ANGEL. It's beautiful, but...

LELAND. It was my mother's. And then Anna... I thought at first we should bury it with her, but my mother said no. Let the dead bury the dead and pass this on to the living.

She hands it back to him.

What's wrong?

ANGEL. I have to tell you something.

LELAND. Are you all right?

ANGEL. I had a miscarriage. I lost the baby.

LELAND. Lost… the baby?

ANGEL. Sam says there was nothing he could do. Sometimes nature takes care of things that weren't supposed to be.

LELAND *sits in the rocking chair and puts his head in his hands. She watches him closely.*

LELAND. I was so happy when Anna told me she was carrying my son. She never had a sick day the whole time she carried him. They still don't know what went wrong. She just stopped breathing in the middle of her labor and by the time they got to him, he wasn't breathing either. They laid them out side by side like they were both just sleeping. (*A beat.*) I'm so sorry. I know how much the baby meant to you. I'm just thankful you're safe.

ANGEL. I'm fine.

LELAND. What did Sam say?

ANGEL. He said I just need to take it easy for a while.

LELAND. Did he say we can try again?

ANGEL. I didn't ask him.

LELAND. Don't you want to?

ANGEL. I can't think about that yet, Leland. It's too soon.

LELAND. I know, but the sooner the better.

ANGEL. Sam said it would be good if I got away for a while. So I wouldn't keep thinking about the baby.

LELAND. That's a good idea. Where should we go?

ANGEL. I don't think that's the kind of trip he meant.

LELAND. What did he mean then?

ANGEL. Just me.

LELAND. You want to take a trip alone?

ANGEL. Well, no. I have a friend to go with me.

LELAND. You're not making any sense.

ANGEL. I want to go to Paris with Guy.

LELAND. To Paris? What are you talking about?

ANGEL. He's... scared to go alone. And I need to get away. Sam says... to get my strength back. We'll get married as soon as I get back. I might even be able to talk Guy into making me a wedding dress.

LELAND. It's because of the babies, isn't it? Because of both my sons dying. (*A beat.*) It was a son, wasn't it?

ANGEL. What difference does it make?

LELAND. I always wanted a son first so he could take care of the younger ones. I always could see myself with a son. (*A beat.*) You don't hold it against me, do you?

ANGEL. Listen to me, Alabama. This isn't about you and it isn't about all the dead mamas and all the dead babies and all the things that are supposed to move me. I'm not that kind of colored woman! I just don't want to think about all that anymore. I'm tired of it! I'm going away. From you. From Harlem. From all those crying colored ghosts who won't shut up and let me live my life!

LELAND. Don't talk like that, Angel! We'll have lots of beautiful babies. I promise.

ANGEL. I don't want any babies. Not yours or anybody's.

A beat.

LELAND. What do you mean?

A beat.

ANGEL. Leave me alone.

LELAND. Tell me what you meant.

ANGEL. Nothing.

LELAND. You're lying.

ANGEL. You want me to lie! That's all you ever wanted. Pretend I'm Anna. Pretend I love you. I'm through with it!

LELAND *grabs her arms and turns her toward him roughly.*

LELAND. Look at me!

ANGEL. I didn't lose the baby. I got rid of it.

LELAND. You got rid of my son? How… (*A beat.*) Dr Thomas?
You let Dr Thomas take my son?

*He grabs her by the shoulders as if to shake her, but he stops
himself and releases her.*

If you didn't have Anna's face, I'd kill you.

He exits. ANGEL *closes and locks the door after him,
leaning against it and closing her eyes wearily.* SAM *enters
downstairs and meets* LELAND *outside the house.*

SAM. Brother Leland…

LELAND. I'm not your brother.

SAM *hears the agitation in* LELAND*'s voice and recognizes
immediately that* LELAND *knows.*

SAM. All right. My mistake.

LELAND. Where are you going?

SAM. Angel… wasn't feeling well. I told her I'd stop by.

LELAND. She's not here.

SAM. Then I guess she's feeling better.

LELAND. Angel told me what you did.

A beat.

SAM. What did she tell you?

LELAND. She told me that you killed my son!

SAM. Go home, man. It's over.

SAM *turns and starts away.* LELAND *pulls a gun from his
belt and points it at* SAM*'s back. There is an immediate
blackout, followed by the sound of one gunshot. In the
darkness, one small spot comes up on* ANGEL*'s horrified
face in the darkness. This spot stays on for just a few seconds
and then the lights go to black.*

Scene Five

Two weeks later. DELIA *enters from her bedroom. She is looking at a newspaper.* GUY *enters from his bedroom. He has a small suitcase which he places by the door. There is a champagne bottle resting in a silver ice bucket with two glasses nearby. He gently turns the bottle.* DELIA *finishes reading the story and folds the paper slowly. She picks up her coat and hat and a small photograph and crosses to Guy's apartment. He is looking at the photograph of Josephine and doesn't notice* DELIA *at first. He looks up and sees her watching him.*

GUY. It's not time to go yet, is it?

DELIA. No. I was just rattling around over there driving myself crazy, so I thought I'd come over here.

GUY. And drive me crazy, too? Well, come on and sit down. I'm trying not to forget anything. I've sent the rest of my luggage ahead and paid the landlord through the end of next month in case… she comes back to get her things.

DELIA. Have you seen the paper?

GUY. Not today.

DELIA (*reads*). 'Murdered physician accused of performing illegal abortion on missing Harlem showgirl.'

GUY. Why do you keep reading that stuff?

DELIA. Everybody in Harlem is reading it!

GUY. Hardly a recommendation!

DELIA. They make it sound so tawdry.

GUY. It is tawdry. And so what? So are we all! Tawdry and tainted and running for our natural lives! (*Sees the photo of Sam.*) You got a picture of Sam. Good.

DELIA. They had one at the hospital. It isn't a very good one. Look how young he is…

GUY. It doesn't matter. He has to be here for the send-off.

DELIA *hands him the photo of Sam, which he props up under the photo of Josephine. He pours a glass of champagne for himself and* DELIA.

Drink up, Sweetie. Sam's spirit requires champagne to ease the journey.

DELIA *turns away.*

Are you okay?

DELIA (*looking at Sam's photo*). We only had a chance to... be together three times... and I just keep thinking about it. I don't even know I'm thinking about it, and there it is. Pictures in my mind and everything. (*A beat.*) I'm sorry... I didn't mean to embarrass you.

GUY. You can't embarrass me.

DELIA. I just didn't know how much I'd miss him. There isn't a single place in Harlem where I don't think about something we did, something he said... (*A beat.*) I thought after the funeral, I'd be able to move on, but...

GUY (*gently*). It's only been a couple of weeks, Sweetie. Give it time.

DELIA. Margaret offered me her place in the mountains. I might just take her up on it.

GUY. Are you serious?

DELIA. Well, you're leaving and the trial isn't for another month at least.

GUY. If you're going away for a month, what's the point of moping around the Catskills? Come with me!

DELIA. To Paris? You're mixing up your lady friends, aren't you?

GUY. Not a chance! Listen to me for a minute. Harlem was supposed to be a place where Negroes could come together and really walk about, and for a red-hot minute, we did. But this isn't the end of the world, you know. It's just New York City.

DELIA. What if Angel comes back?

A beat.

GUY. When I first met Angel at Miss Lillie's, she was already saving her getaway money. She had her little coins and crumpled-up dollar bills all knotted up in somebody's great big silk handkerchief. She was headed up to Harlem as fast as she could get there and she believed it so hard, I believed it, too. So I got my own white silk handkerchief and started putting those coins in there every day and counting them every night. And I'd be lying there with my eyes closed, letting those old men touch me wherever they felt like it, but it didn't matter, because in my mind, I was stomping at the Savoy! But I never told Angel. I just kept my ears open so when she was ready to make a move, I'd be ready too. One of the other girls told me she was leaving one night late, so I got my little suitcase and met her at the train station. She was happy to see me, but she sure would have left without me. (*A beat*.) Angel doesn't like to say goodbye.

DELIA. I want her to say she's sorry.

GUY. Sorry ain't worth waiting for, trust me. All sorry can do is sit there. It can't ever make it right. We got our hearts broken, Deal, but we don't have to pay for it with our lives. Sam already took care of those dues.

DELIA. I don't even have a ticket!

GUY. Do you have a passport?

DELIA. Yes, but…

GUY. It's never crowded this time of year. We can book your passage at the dock. I've got plenty of money and a huge stateroom. If worse comes to worse, we'll tell them you're my little sister and you can bunk with me.

DELIA. I can't just pick up and… what about the clinic?

GUY. Don't tell me those suffragettes down there can't figure out what to do for a couple of weeks without you!

DELIA. I'm not even packed.

GUY. We'll buy you whatever you need on the ship! Including a new hat!

DELIA. I love this hat!

GUY. I know!

He opens the door and grabs his suitcase.

Ready?

She clearly wants to go, but she hesitates, amazed at her own boldness.

DELIA. Can I really do this?

GUY. What would Sam say?

She hesitates, then smiles slowly.

DELIA. Let the good times roll!

GUY. Then get your passport and meet me at the corner! I'll get us a cab.

DELIA. I won't be a minute!

GUY. You better not be! We're going first-class, but I don't think they'll hold the ship for us.

He exits quickly. DELIA *goes over to her apartment, rummages quickly through her desk looking for her passport, doesn't find it. She stops, thinks, then exits to the bedroom. A beat.* ANGEL *enters cautiously through the back door, listens to be sure they have gone and then lets herself into Guy's apartment, leaving the door open behind her. The two champagne glasses are still there. Sam's picture is still propped under the photo of Josephine. She picks the photo up and stands looking at it quietly.*

DELIA *comes out of her bedroom with her passport and a small overnight bag. She is moving rapidly. She moves into the hallway and sees Guy's open door, stops, enters cautiously.* ANGEL, *still holding the picture of Sam, looks up and sees her standing there. In that moment, both understand that things have changed forever between them.* ANGEL *crosses to* DELIA *and hands her the photograph.* DELIA *takes it.*

ANGEL. Goodbye, Deal.

DELIA. Goodbye, Angel.

DELIA *exits quickly without looking back.* ANGEL *looks around the apartment slowly and sees her fan still in its usual place near the window. She picks up the fan, walks to the open window and sits down, looking out calmly in a moment that is clearly reminiscent of the afternoon she first encountered Leland walking by her window. She has been faced with these same difficult decisions about how she will live many times and although she would have avoided this moment if she could have figured out how, she is not in a state of panic or confusion or even remorse. She is thinking, figuring out what is, and what is next. A respectable-looking* MAN *in a nice suit enters, walking with a sense of purpose until he sees* ANGEL *sitting in the window at the same moment she sees him. He keeps walking, but then slows, stops and turns back to her. She smiles, fanning herself slowly.*

ANGEL. Hot enough for you?

Lights to black.